The
Scots-Irish
in the
Hills of Tennessee

by

BILLY KENNEDY

 auseway
PRESS

 AMBASSADOR
PRODUCTIONS

The Scots-Irish in the Hills of Tennessee
© 1995 Billy Kennedy

First published June 1995
Second edition, September 1995
Third edition, December 1995
This edition, September 1996

THE
SCOTS-IRISH CHRONICLES

Scots-Irish in the Hills of Tennessee

Scots-Irish in the Shenandoah Valley

Cover: The Frontierman painting by David Wright, Nashville.
Sarah Polk (top left), Davy Crockett (top right),
Rachel Jackson (bottom left) and Andrew Jackson (bottom right).

ISBN 1 898787 46 8

Published by

Causeway Press
9, Ebrington Terrace,
Londonderry, BT47 1JS

Ambassador Productions
16, Hillview Avenue,
Belfast, BT5 6JR

Emerald House Group Inc.
1 Chick Springs Road, Suite 206
Greenville, South Carolina 29609

About *the Author*

BILLY KENNEDY is assistant editor of the Ulster/Belfast News Letter, Northern Ireland's leading morning newspaper and the oldest English language newspaper, having been founded in 1737. He was born in Belfast in 1943, but has spent almost his entire life living in Co. Armagh. He comes of Scots-Irish Presbyterian roots and has a deep fascination for his forebears of that tradition who moved to America in such large numbers during the 18th century. For the past 25 years, Billy Kennedy has been one of the leading journalists in Northern Ireland, covering the major stories of the Ulster troubles and as a prolific columnist on a variety of issues. He was a news editor with the News Letter for 18 years and in his present capacity as assistant editor of the newspaper, he is a leader writer and is also religious affairs and local government correspondent. He is an authority on American country music and culture and has interviewed for the News Letter Nashville personalities such as Garth Brooks, George Jones, Willie Nelson, Charley Pride, Ricky Skaggs and Reba McEntire. For research on this book he travelled extensively through Tennessee over a two-year period and met and talked with many Tennesseans with direct links to the Scots-Irish settlers of 200 years ago. Billy Kennedy is also a specialist on sport and for 30 years he has written and compiled various publications for soccer internationally and on the local domestic football scene in Northern Ireland. He has edited and compiled books on cultural traditions in Ireland, including two on the history of Orangeism in Ireland. He is married with a grown-up daughter.

Dedication

*This book is dedicated to
my loving wife Sally, daughter Julie
and my parents.*

Billy Kennedy

*"Oh that my words were now written; Oh
that they were printed in a book. That they
were graven with an iron pen and lead in
the rock for ever. For I know that my
Redeemer liveth and that He shall stand
at the latter day upon the earth."*
Job Ch. 19 verses 23-25.

~.~

*The author acknowledges the help and support
given to him in the compilation of this book by
Samuel Lowry of Ambassador Productions and
Gregory Campbell of Causeway Press. It was
wholeheartedly a team effort!*

List *of Contents*

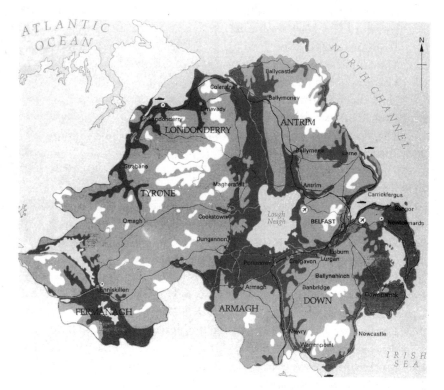

Map of Northern Ireland

Cover Painting: *The Frontiersman*

They came over the mountains - to explore, to hunt, to trap. These men we refer to as the long hunters, the frontiersmen, overmountain men all shared one common trait: they sought their existence from the wilderness. They explored that dangerous expanse of land between the Appalachian Mountains and the Mississippi River.

Prior to the growth of the western fur trade in the early 1800s, the frontiersman had already explored that land referred to as "Kaintuck" and other surrounding areas. The Shawnee, Chickasaw and Cherokee were Indians he traded with and fought against.

I chose to locate my subject in the Appalachian Mountains, as he overlooks that expanse of land that was "his" - in the sense that he took what he needed and moved on, leaving the land as he had found it. Later, he brought people to settle it.

I have found myself, when deer hunting here in Tennessee, seeking a high point just to look out over the land. In the more remote areas I find a great satisfaction in surveying my surroundings - the woods, the hills-unbroken by the crowded habitat of man. I can imagine this same desire in man at all times in history.

I suppose my painting of The Frontiersman may be more symbolic than factually representational. The gun, accoutrements and clothing are carefully researched. However, he may be a bit cleaner, better dressed than your average frontiersman of the day. I wanted this portrait to represent the heroic efforts, whether good or bad, of those men who played such an important part in the settling of our country. Maybe you, the viewer, won't think too unkindly of me for wanting to portray the frontiersman in this way.

David Wright,
Nashville.

• The author acknowledges with thanks David Wright's gesture in allowing his painting "The Frontiersman" to be used as the cover for this book.

Hi! Uncle Sam!
  When freedom was denied you,
And Imperial might defied you,
  Who was it stood beside you
At Quebec and Brandywine?
  And dared retreats and dangers,
Redcoats and Hessian strangers,
  In the lean, long-rifled Rangers,
And the Pennsylvania Line!

Hi! Uncle Sam!
  Wherever there was fighting,
Or wrong that needed righting,
  An Ulsterman was sighting
His Kentucky gun with care:
  All the road to Yorktown,
From Lexington to Yorktown,
  From Valley Forge to Yorktown,
That Ulsterman was there!

Hi! Uncle Sam!
  Virginia sent her brave men,
The North paraded grave men,
  That they might not be slave men,
But ponder this with calm:
  The first to face the Tory,
And the first to lift Old Glory
  Made your war an Ulster story:
Think it over, Uncle Sam!

W. F. Marshall (Rev),
Co. Tyrone

Foreword *from Tennessee*

Dr. John Rice Irwin

Few people in America have been so romanticised, discussed and analysed as have those Scotch-Irish who settled generally in the Southern Appalachian Mountains of the United States, and in the Tennessee mountains in particular. Almost everyone, it seems, who has written about this region refers admirably to the Scotch-Irish as a brave, hard working, independent, self-reliant, and fiercely honest people. These phrases often became repetitious to the extent that one wondered if there was a basis in fact for this repeated refrain.

As a child growing up in a rural isolated section of the East Tennessee mountains, I wondered why the old folks, with whom I spent so much of my time, never talked about their European origins. They were a colorful, jolly lot, and they, of all people, were wont to tell stories about their families, about the wild and romantic frontier their fathers and mothers tamed. They were reflective, philosophical, and even studious when it came to unwritten history; but in referring to the "old" family members they never got beyond Virginia, North Carolina or possibly Pennsylvania.

I never heard a family member nor a neighbour talk of someone being English, German, Italian, Scotch-Irish, or anything else. Having reflected on this for years I've concluded that because of generations of migration, the continuing flow of lore and stories of ancestry was almost totally broken. There was little or no contact with parents, and most often there was none at all with grandparents. So, we were all Americans, and if pushed as to where one's family was from, the family patriarch might say "they was Irish or they was Scotch-Irish", or that "they came from across the waters".

I often wondered, about our ancestors who were the Scotch-Irish. Why did they leave Northern Ireland, how many came, why, and what was their role in developing America after they came here? I pondered the questions for years, and it was Billy Kennedy, in his insightful manner, who addressed this and other thought provoking questions in a most impressive manner. Through the historical treaties and biographies of so many great Scotch-Irish Americans, he has placed meat on the bones of the often hollow sounding phrases describing the Scotch-Irish as "independent, self-reliant, God-fearing honest, fierce, loyal etc . . . "

Billy Kennedy came here and he saw us as we had not, and could not, see ourselves, And he's made us more proud of our Scotch-Irish ancestry than we had been before. Moreover he's instilled a bit of pride among the population of Northern Ireland whose kin contributed so very much to the forging of what Kennedy himself calls the greatest nation in the world.

Billy Kennedy's unbounded enthusiasm for his task, his substantive research, and his love for his kin, permeates every page of this book. It is much more than a study of the influence and contributions of one group of people. It is, in reality, a most revealing introduction to the history of the United States of America. What better way is there to know and understand a country then to know and understand the interesting, colorful, and personal lives of those men and women who helped to develop that country?

What better way is there to understand a nation than to know and understand the people who were instrumental in building that nation; and what better way is there to understand a people than to study the nation they helped to create.

Dr. John Rice Irwin,
Founder and Director, Museum of Appalachia,
Norris, Tennessee.

John Rice Irwin is founder and director of the Museum of Appalachia in Norris, Tennessee, a farm-village settlement which has gained publicity and acclaim throughout the United States. He is a former college, university and public school teacher and has served as both school principal and county school superintendent. He has also engaged successfully in farming, real estate, Appalachian Music (he has his own eight member string band), and several small businesses and corporations which he started.

John Rice's main interest, however, lies in the people of his native Southern Appalachian Mountains. Since childhood he has spent virtually all his spare time visiting and talking with these mountain folk whom he admires and loves. He is considered to be one of the leading authorities on the history, culture, and people of Southern Appalachia, and on American pioneer-frontier life in general.

John Rice Irwin is a prolific author, having written five books on life in the Southern Appalachian region:
• Musical Instruments of the Southern Appalachian Mountains. - 1979
• Guns and Gunmaking, Tools of Southern Appalachia. -1980
• Baskets and Basket Making in Southern Appalachia. - 1982
• A People and Their Quilts. - 1983
• Alex Stewart, Portrait of a Pioneer, - 1985
These books are published by Schiffer Publishing, West Chester, Pennsylvania.

Born in 1930 of pioneer ancestors of a Scots-Irish and Welsh lineage, John Rice Irwin spent much of his childhood with his grandparents learning to love all aspects of Appalachian life and its colourful people. He joined the US Infantry during the Korean War and served two years. He has a degree in history and economics and a masters degree in international law.

John Rice Irwin has featured in dozens of national magazine articles (from Reader's Digest to Parade to Southern Living), thousands of newspaper stories, and featured in over a dozen nationally viewed TV documentaries.

He was chosen as "Citizen of the Year" in 1988 in his hometown of Norris and in 1989 was selected as one of 29 MacArthur Fellows in America, one of his country's most prestigious awards.

He was the subject of a one-hour TV movie which was a year in the making, produced by the Parson's Foundation of Los Angeles.

He received the 1992 "Outstanding Marketing Professional" award presented by the Knoxville Chapter of the American Marketing Association and was awarded an honorary doctorate degree in Humane Letters from Cumberland College, Williamsburg, Kentucky in 1993 and an honorary doctorate of Humanities from Lincoln Memorial University, Harrogate, Tennessee in 1994.

Foreword *from Northern Ireland*

Dr. Ian Adamson

S et as Ulster is at the North Eastern corner of Ireland, facing the British mainland across a narrow sea and separated from the rest of Ireland by a zone of little hills known as drumlins, the characteristics of her language and people have been moulded by movements, large and small between the two islands since the dawn of human history.

P. L. Henry has described the difference between Ulster and the rest of Ireland as: "One of the most deeply rooted ancient, and from a literary point of view, most productive facts of early Irish history." Furthermore, "Ulster's bond with Scotland counterbalances her lax tie with the rest of Ireland. To say, once more, that this applies only to modern times and to dialects of English would be to miscalculate most grossly. Here too the mould was fixed in ancient times and modern developments continue ancient associations. We need but think of the Pictish (Cruthin or British) Kingdoms in both areas, of the Ulster-Scottish Kingdom of Dalriada from the last quarter of the fifth century to the close of the eighth century, of the Scottish Kingdom founded under gaelic leadership in 842, of Irish relations with the Kingdom of the Hebrides and Argyll from the 12th century, particularly the immigration of Hebridean soldiers (Gallowglasses) from the 13th to the 16th century.

"The Gaelic form of this word, Galloglaigh, (i.e. Gallagher) occurs as a family name in Northern Ireland. There was a constant coming and going between North East Ireland and Western Scotland. The Glens of Antrim were in the hands of Scottish Macdonalds by 1400, and for the next 200 years Gaelic-speaking Scots came in large numbers. The 17th century immigration of a numerous Scots element need not be considered outside the preceding series. It has brought for example Presbyterian Scots with names as familiar on this side as McMennemin and Kennedy, who must be considered rather in the light of homing birds."[1]

In the following century, however, the people of Ulster were to make another great migration, and that was to be to a New World. Pressured by Southern gaelic expansion into Scotland earlier in the Christian era, many had returned to the lands of their ancestors. In speech, in temper, in outlook, the Ulster people contrasted more sharply with the natives of the other provinces of Ireland than the English midlands with the Home counties. In America they became known as Scotch-Irish.

Although the Scotch-Irish merged quickly into the American nation, the Ulster speech itself was to stay alive in the hill-country of Appalachia and beyond, where Scots-Irish traditional music may still be heard. Among the earliest songs were ballads of King William of Orange, so those who sung them became known as Billy-boys of the hill-country or "hillbillies". Rooted deep in the traditions of the British Isles peasantry, the fiddle had become an instrument of major importance in the development of Irish, Scottish and Welsh jigs, reels and hornpipes. As with folk custom in general, traditional music themes reinforced the ancient cultural divide between North/West Britain and Ireland, and South and Eastern Britain.

Transposed to America, the hoedown fiddle reached the peak of its development in the Southern States. In the latter half of the 1880s came the fiddle-banjo duet and in the early 1900s the fiddle, banjo and guitar trio was formed in the Southern mountains. Soon other forms of popular music, such as ragtime and jazz, had their effect on the mountain music. Different styles of fiddling developed, the most important perhaps being that of the Blues fiddling typified by the Mississippi Sheiks. This style, predominant in the deep South, was one of the richest contributions of the Black people to American life, not only for itself but because of its effect on such Florida fiddlers as Chubby Wise. Playing with Bill Monroe, Wise formulated a new sound which was to become known as Bluegrass.

Musicologist W. H. Williams has written: "Ireland's initial impact upon American music came predominantly from Ulster . . ." Whatever their influence in terms of cabin and barn styles, field layout, town planning, and so on, it seems likely that the greatest and most lasting contribution of the Scotch-Irish was music. And however one may define their particular religious and ethnic identity, musically they should be considered Ulstermen, for they brought with them the mixture of Scottish and Irish tunes which is still characteristic of large parts of Northern Ireland. When the great English folklorist Cecil Sharp went into the Appalachians to rediscover "English" folk song, he was in fact often dealing with people of Ulster descent. Wherever they settled in large numbers and remained in relative isolation, balladry has been found live and in a healthy condition.[2]

There are many modern Americans who still take pride in their descent from Ulster-Irish families, though they often know little of Ulster per se. Not many of these are now Presbyterian, for most became Methodists and Baptists according to conscience. This was due to old-time preachers whose traditions also live on in the American Black community. The National Opinion Research Centre at the University of Chicago had indeed introduced statistics which demonstrated that 12 per cent of adult Americans named Ireland as the country from which most of their ancestors came and 56 per cent of these belonged to one of the Protestant churches. Very little about the Ulster contribution to America is taught, however, in our schools and universities. Harold R. Alexander has written : "The migration of the Ulster people was a diaspora similar to that of the Jews. North America provided ample scope for the national character and soaring vision of men of Ulster origin. It is sad that almost nothing of this is known in Ulster today. English ascendancy and Irish chauvinism have combined to suppress knowledge of Ulster and Ulster-American history, to deny the very concept of the Ulster nation at home or overseas and to deprive Ulstermen of legitimate pride in their heritage and national identity."[3]

I feel immensely proud to have been asked by Billy Kennedy to write a foreword to his fine new book, filled with fascinating insights into the lives of the early pioneers and patriots of the United States. This book provides a fund of information about the Ulster diaspora. For Americans it will act as a link between their homeland and their ancient roots in Scotland and Ireland. For Ulster people everywhere it will serve as a timely reminder of their place in history and the significant part they have played in shaping the destiny of the world.

Dr. Ian Adamson,
M.B., B.Ch., B.A.O. (Q.U.B.), D.C.H.., R.C.P.S. (Glasgow)
D.C.H., R.C.S. (Dublin), M.F.C.H.
Deputy Lord Mayor of Belfast.
June 1, 1995

Footnotes

1. Henry, P. L. "Ulster Dialects", Ulster Folk Museum, 1964.
2. Williams, W. H. A., "Irish Traditional Music in the United States" America and Ireland: 1776-1976, Greenwood Press, U.S.A. 1980.
3. Alexander, Harold R., The Mecklenburg Declaration of Independence, Ulster Heritagem, Glenolden, PA, 1978

Books by Dr. Ian Adamson:
The Cruthin (1974)
Bangor, Light of the World (1979)
The Battle of Moira (1980)
The Identity of Ulster (1982)
The Ulster People (1991)
Published by Pretani Press, 78 Abbey Street, Bangor, BT20 4JB, Northern Ireland

1

Tennessee *and its Ulster links*

About one in five Tennesseans today can trace their roots back to the Scots-Irish settlers of 200-250 years ago. This is confirmed in the 1990 figures for selective social characteristics for the state of Tennessee, conducted by the United States Department of Commerce, Bureau of Census. These established that 197,942 were of Scots-Irish ancestry, 100,080 Scottish and 875,771 Irish. Accepting that the vast majority of the Irish settlers in Tennessee came from Ulster (north of Ireland) stock and were of Protestant/Presbyterian vintage, the figure of one million present-day Tennesseans in the Scots-Irish tradition is an accurate assessment.

Tennessee, with its forests, lakes and mountains is similar in its geographical landscape to Ireland and Scotland, with the greenery just as pronounced. The state has five main regions: the Middle Tennessee heartland around Nashville - Music City USA and its surrounding horse country of Maury, Sumner and Davidson Counties; the Plateaux and Valley centred on Chattanooga and an area of rivers and lakes; the mountainous east linking Knoxville, the Tennessee Valley and the Great Smoky Mountains; the Delta Country towards blues capital Memphis in the west and the first frontier, the north eastern area where the first settlers - mainly the Scots-Irish - moved in at the end of the 18th Century.

Memphis (population 610,000), Nashville (500,000), Knoxville (165,000), Chattanooga (155,000), Clarksville (75,000) and Johnson City (50,000) are the main population centres in this state of five million. The other settlements in the 95 Tennessean counties are essentially well-ordered small rural towns, with populations no larger than 50,000. The furthest point in the state is 500 miles.

Northern *Ireland*

Northern Ireland, an integral part of the United Kingdom, has a population of 1.6 million and its geographical boundary takes in six of the nine counties of the Irish province of Ulster. The majority of the people in Northern Ireland, almost two-thirds, are Protestant and British by culture and tradition, are committed to maintaining the constitutional link with the British Crown.

Just over one-third of the population is Roman Catholic, most of whom are Irish by culture and tradition and seek the re-unification of Ireland through a link-up with the Irish Republic. A sizeable number of Roman Catholics in Northern Ireland are known to favour maintaining the status quo link with Britain, therefore it is wrong to look at the political breakdown through a sectarian headcount.

The one million Protestants in Northern Ireland are descendants of Scottish and English settlers who moved from the British mainland in the 17th and 18th centuries. Presbyterians, who formed the bulk of those who moved to the American frontier lands in the 18th century, are to-day the most numerous Protestant tradition in Northern Ireland, totalling 400,000. The Church of Ireland (Anglican Episcopal) community account for 350,000 people, Methodists 70,000 with smaller Protestant denominations accounting for the rest.

Belfast (population 500,000) is the capital of Northern Ireland and the six counties are Antrim, Down, Londonderry, Tyrone, Armagh and Fermanagh. The main exodus of the Scots-Irish Presbyterians came from four of these counties: Antrim, Down, Tyrone and Londonderry and from Donegal, one of the Ulster counties in the Republic of Ireland.

2

The Scots-Irish: *a sturdy independent breed of people*

The Scots-Irish are a people who originated in lowland Scotland, moved to the north of Ireland during the 17th century and emigrated to America in large numbers throughout the 18th century. The overwhelming number of the Scots-Irish emigrants to the American frontier lands were Presbyterians, a sturdy independent breed whose courage and dynamic work ethic became imprinted on the landscape of what was to become the greatest nation on earth.

Between 1717 and the American Revolutionary War years of the late 1770s and early 1780s an estimated quarter of a million Scots-Irish settlers left the province of Ulster in the northern part of Ireland for the new lands across the Atlantic. They travelled in extremely hazardous conditions, in wooden sailing ships from the Ulster ports of Belfast, Larne, Londonderry, Newry and Portrush for the far-off berths of Philadelphia, New Castle (Delaware), Charleston, Baltimore and New York. Huddled together with the most meagre of belongings and money, they were a people forced to move because of the severe restrictions placed on their faith by the ruling British establishment of the day and because of the economic deprivations prevailing in their Ulster homeland.

The Scots-Irish Presbyterians who headed west 200-250 years ago belonged to the same race of people who today constitute the majority Protestant and Unionist community in Northern Ireland. Virtually all of these emigrants were so embittered by the discriminatory practices levelled against them by the offices of the Crown that they led the vanguard against the British in the War of Independence in America.

In Northern Ireland today the Scots-Irish (the Protestant-Unionist population) pledge themselves to the maintenance of the link with Britain, but the complexities of the several hundred years of British history fully explain this paradoxical situation in terms of economic benefit and cultural attachments for the one million people who presently hold firm to this view.

In the United States today an estimated 40 million people claim Irish extraction. But while the Irish American community, the descendants of the Roman Catholic emigrants who moved at the time of the potato famine in the mid-19th century, are the most vocal and politically active on Ireland, 56 per cent of Americans with Irish roots are of Protestant stock, whose forebears were the Scots-Irish Presbyterians who settled on the frontier in the 18th century.

Civil and religious liberty had been established in the British Isles by King William III through the Glorious Revolution of 1688-89 and the Scottish planters who had settled in Ulster appeared to be getting a better deal for their dissenting religious beliefs.

Over a 100-year period from about 1610 the Scots had moved in large numbers to the counties of Antrim, Down, Londonderry, Tyrone and Donegal; they had worked the farms, established industry with French Huguenot Protestants who had fought with King William in his battles and erected meeting houses for their Presbyterian form of worship, and schools for the education of their children. In Presbyterian minds, the church and the school are inter-twinned and this was the case when the Scots-Irish arrived in America.

William's reign ended in 1702 and when his cousin Anne ascended the throne a High Anglican Church faction became dominant in government in London and enacted legislation which weighed heavily on the minds and consciences of the Presbyterians of Ulster. An Act was passed in 1703 which required all office holders in Ireland to take the sacrament according to the requirements of the Established Episcopal Church. As many Presbyterians held posts as magistrates and civic duties under the Crown they were automatically disqualified unless they renounced the dissenting Calvinistic faith of their forefathers in Scotland.

Members of the Roman Catholic Church who in the main constituted the native Irish population in Ireland also bore the brunt of the discriminatory Test Act. But in the administering of religion Roman Catholic priests were at least recognised by the High Churchmen as being lawfully ordained.

Presbyterian ministers were in no such position and right across Ulster they were turned out of their pulpits and threatened with legal proceedings should they defy the edict from London. Ministers had no official standing and were unable to sanctify marriage; unable to officiate at the burial of one of their congregation and prevented from teaching children in schools on any aspect of the Presbyterian faith.

This narrow piece of legislation left the Presbyterian population, by then a highly significant section of the Ulster community, deeply resentful and almost totally alienated from their political masters in the Established Church. The Act had the effect of making the Presbyterian people speak increasingly of starting a new life in America. Their protests had been ignored and there was unanimity from the pulpit to the pew that this may be the only way to ease the suffering.

The harsh economics of life in Ireland in the early 18th century was another factor which made immigration more appealing. Four years of drought made life almost unbearable for the small peasant farmers on the hillsides of Ulster and, with the High Church landlords staking claims to exhorbitant rents and the textile industry in recession, the movement of the Scots-Irish to America began in earnest.

The first ships were chartered in 1717 and in that year, when drought completely ruined the crops on the Ulster farmlands, 5,000 men and women headed to Pennsylvania. There were five great waves of immigration to America from Ulster in the 18th century: 1717-18, 1725-29, 1740-41, 1754-55 and 1771-75. The first wave prompted Archbishop of Canterbury William King to censure Parliament over its discriminatory laws and, another High Churchman Dean Jonathan Swift spoke out against the iniquitous rack-renting (the raising of rents to ridiculous figures) which was prevalent at the time.

The migration of 1725-29 was so large that it forced the Government in London to sit up at last and take notice. Parliament, worried by the decrease in numbers of the Protestant population in Ulster, appointed a commission to investigate the causes of movement. Rack-renting was given as the main reason for the second wave: the religious restriction still applied, but poverty had taken its toll and the promise of a better life in the new world proved irresistible.

It was an Ulsterman placed high in the seat of Government in Pennsylvania who welcomed the first waves of settlers to America. James Logan, born in Lurgan, Co. Armagh, was Provincial Secretary and at first he looked upon the emigrants as his "brave fellow-countrymen". He wrote in 1720: "At the time we were apprehensive of the Northern Indians. I therefore thought it would be prudent to plant a settlement of such men as those who formerly had so bravely defended Londonderry and Inniskillen as a frontier in case of any disturbance. These people, if kindly used, will be orderly as they have hitherto been and easily dealt with. They will, I expect, be a leading example to others".

Logan, a close associate of the Quaker William Penn, gave the new settlers an extensive tract of land in Chester (now Lancaster) County and the first settlement bore the name of Donegal. However, within a decade Logan, a Quaker and a pacifist himself, felt less disposed to the Scots-Irish who were flooding on to America's shores. He still admired their indominable courage, but found they exhibited belligerent uncompromising traits which were offensive to him.

He wrote that "a settlement of five families from the north of Ireland give me more trouble than 50 of any other people". And added: "It looks as if Ireland is to send all her inhabitants hither, for last week not less than six ships arrived, and every day two or three arrive also. The common fear is that if they continue to come they will make themselves proprietors of the province".

Logan admitted the Scots-Irish were "troublesome settlers to the government and hard neighbours to the Indians". Many settled on land without bothering to secure legal rights for it - the practice of squatting had begun and would spread like wildfire across the frontier for the next 100 years.

The Irish famine of 1740-41 led to the third great wave of immigration to America by the Scots-Irish. An estimated 400,000 people perished in that famine and when the Presbyterian settlers arrived in America they set their sights beyond the borders of Pennsylvania - along the path of the Great Valley to the Shenandoah region of Virginia and to South and North Carolina. In the period between 1728 and 1750 it was estimated Ulster lost a quarter of her trading cash and about a quarter of her population engaged in manufacture, as a result of the migration to America. This underlined the seriousness of the movement.

The 1754-55 exodus resulted from appeals by colonists in America to settle on the new lands of Virginia and South and North Carolina and from another calamitous drought in Ireland. Thousands headed out, despite a relative improvement in economic conditions back home, and it was during these years that the Scots-Irish came into direct conflict with the Indian tribes.

In the last great wave of 1771-75, land leases were cited as the main bone of contention, with the Marquis of Donegall in Co. Antrim being a very unpopular landlord for the demands he was making on the small peasant farmers, and for the evictions he so callously implemented. Not enough ships could be found to carry the throng of Presbyterians eager to go ..... in the two years that followed the evictions in Co. Antrim no fewer than 30,000 Presbyterians left Ulster. It was recorded at the time: "Almost all of them emigrated at their own charge: a great majority of them were persons employed in the linen manufacture or farmers possessed by property which they converted into money and carried with them".

For 50 years after 1775, many more Ulster-Scots emigrated, but the numbers did not match those in the 58 years of the Great Migration. Historian of the period Arthur Young wrote: "The spirit of emigrating in Ireland in the 18th century appeared to be confined to two circumstances, the Presbyterian religion and the decline of the linen industry. Catholics never went; they seem not only tied to the country, but almost to the parish in which their ancestors lived; and members of the Established Church rarely went". Another historian James Froude said the migration from Ulster "robbed Ireland of the bravest defenders of the English interests and peopled the American seaboard with fresh flights of Puritans".

Next to the English, the Scots-Irish by the end of the 18th century became the most influential section of the white population in America, which, by 1790, numbered 3,172,444. At that time, the Scots-Irish segment of the population totalled about 14 per cent and this figure was much higher in the Appalachian states of Virginia, Tennessee, Kentucky and North Carolina.

Over half a century the Ulster-Scots and their off-spring progressed from being immigrant settlers to become naturalised Americans, totally assimilated in the fabric of their new nation. Their involvement in the

War of Independence made the Scots-Irish think less of their old country and more of the lush fertile lands that were opening up in front of them. As they pioneered the Carolinas, Virginia, and the new states of Kentucky and Tennessee they were increasingly doing so as Americans, not as Irish or Scots.

Kentucky became a state in 1792 and Tennessee in 1796 and it is significant that, while the Scots-Irish were a highly-populous community in both these regions, their ethnic or national background (racial stock) has never been recorded to any large degree. This is because the first settlers in Kentucky had stressed their movement from Virginia and Tennessee and from North and South Carolina rather than the far distant lands their parents and grandparents had left. Their religion and their cultural characteristics indicated who they were, but their assimilation with other American people no longer made them a distinctive ethnic group.

The movement *from Ulster*

The first recorded sailing of an emigrant passenger ship from Ulster to America was that of 'The Friends' Goodwill' which left Larne in Co. Antrim for Boston in April 1717. Five thousand people left Ulster that year for America, laying the foundations for future immigration and settlement.

Those who made the break for the New World did so at a great price. Almost one in three of the Ulster Presbyterians who sailed to America did so under contracts of service or indenture as it was more commonly known. Contracts for terms of between four and seven years were most common and reflected the great need that existed in the colonies for hired help.

The Ulster settlers tended to settle together and mixed little with the English and Germans already there. Poverty also forced them from the more expensive land in the east to the frontier regions, where land was cheap and readily available; other simply squatted in defiance of the authorities.

There were, however, drawbacks, none more so than the risk of being attacked by Indians. Colonial officials were glad to have the Ulster people to provide a buffer against hostile natives. When trouble arose, the Scots-Irish settlers were left to their fate, an experience which hardened and embittered them against the British Government, just as had been the case back home in Ulster.

It is generally acknowledged that the Revolutionary War for independence in America in the 1770s was essentially a dispute between the Scots-Irish immigrants and the Crown, especially in the Appalachian region. In some states in 1776, the Ulster-Scots population was at least one-third.

From Pennsylvania, the Ulster settlement spread along the Valley of Virginia during the 1730s and 1740s following the Great Philadelphia Wagon Road. This was the famous 'back country' where their presence was welcomed as a reinforcement against the Indian threat. Most of the movement into North Carolina took place between 1740 and 1756, with the surge into South Carolina developing in the 1760s. The move into East Tennessee developed about 1770-1780.

By the time the Revolutionary War came, about 90 per cent of the Ulster settlers had made their homes in Pennsylvania, the Valley of Virginia and the Carolinas. The Ulster settlers became quite a formidable force. Abandoned to their fate by their British masters, who had let them down so many times in the past, the Ulstermen and women began to feel themselves American above everything else. Ulster families were in the vanguard of the push west. Moving across the mountain barriers, many would leave Virginia for Kentucky, or North Carolina for Tennessee, while many others migrated from eastern Pennsylvania into the Ohio Valley.

President Theodore Roosevelt paid this fulsome tribute to this remarkable chapter in American history: "The backswoodsmen were American by birth and parentage, and of mixed race; but the dominate strain in their blood was that of the Presbyterian-Irish, the Scots-Irish as they were often called. These Irish representatives of the Covenanters were in the west almost what the Puritans were in the north-east, and more than the Cavaliers were in the south. Mingled with the descendants of many other races, they nevertheless formed the kernel of the distinctively and intensely American stock who were the pioneers of our people in their march westward, the vanguard of the army of fighting settlers, who with axe and rifle won their way ... to the Rio Grande and the Pacific."

The Ulstermen and women were natural frontiersmen, their character was shaped by the frontier into something new, the characteristic which today is recognised as American.

3

The Scots-Irish *(Scotch-Irish) designation*

Scots-Irish is the modern term used to describe the people who settled in the American frontier in the 100 years from about 1717. These settlers were overwhelmingly Presbyterian whose forebears had originally been lowland Scots who arrived in the north of Ireland (the province of Ulster and today Northern Ireland) in the early 17th century.

Some in the United States today refer to the "Scotch-Irish", but this term now causes offence to many of the Scots-Irish tradition in Britain and America where "Scotch" is looked upon as an alcoholic spirit. In Northern Ireland the designation Ulster-Scot is very widely used by the Presbyterian descendants of the early frontier settlers. Nevertheless, for all the sensitivities it still touches upon, the term "Scotch-Irish" has an historical reality and utility. Ulsterman Francis Mackemie (Makemie), the founding father of the Presbyterian Church in America, was enrolled in the University of Glasgow in February, 1676 as "Franciscus Makemus Scoto-Hyburnus".

The form"Scotch-Irish" would have been used in the vernacular, as "Scotch" was the proper idiom until the 20th century for both language and people. "Scotch-Irish" had been used for the Ulster-Scots in America as early as 1695, but usually in a figurative way. The early Presbyterians from Ireland generally knew themselves simply as "Irish" and were thus known by the other colonists. The later establishment and rapid growth of highly visible Irish Roman Catholic communities led many Protestants in the United States to adopt the Scotch-Irish label.

Popular identification with the term, particularly among the educated and ambitious, reached its zenith in the United States in the 1890s. "Scotch-Irish" was also the term used by the world's foremost authority on the Ulster-Scots language, Professor Robert J. Gregg, of the University of British Colombia, for those dialects originally known as "Scotch" which were spoken by the 17th century settlers in Ulster. These dialects were modified in the mouths of the local Gaelic speakers who acquired them and eventually, after a bilingual period, lost their native tongue. The modified dialects were then gradually adopted by the Scottish and Engish settlers themselves, since the Irish constituted the majority population "Scotch-Irish" (Ulster-Scots). Although a closely related, sibling language to English it is, however, strikingly different to English in phonology and morphology.

Michael Montgomery, of the University of South Carolina, has traced the Scotch-Irish element in Appalachian English. His study strongly suggests that the Scotch-Irish influence on Appalachian English, at least on its grammar, was broad in terms of the variety and deep in terms of the number of patterns. It indicates as well that many Appalachian features contributed by Ulster emigrants continue to thrive in modern-day speech, that they were not levelled away.

4

How the Scots-Irish *were viewed*

They were the first to proclaim for freedom in these United States: even before Lexington the Scots-Irish blood had been shed for American freedom. In the forefront of every battle was seen their burnished mail and in the rear of retreat was heard their voice of constancy" - **President William McKinley** in a speech at Springfield, Ohio May 11, 1893.

"If defeated everywhere else, I will make my stand for liberty among the Scots-Irish of my native Virginia" - **General George Washington**, who throughout the Revolutionary War showed his high regard for the American troops of Ulster origin. Washington was impressed by the Ulster tenacity of spirit, the Ulster determination to see a thing right through to the end.

"We have lost America through the Irish" - **Lord Mountjoy** in the British House of Commons.

"I hear that our American cousin has run away with a Scots-Irish parson" - British Prime Minister **Horace Walpole** in a jibe to his cabinet.

"It is doubtful if we have fully realised the part played by this stern and virile people. They formed the kernal of that American stock who were the pioneers of our people in the march westward. They were a bold and hardy people who pushed past the settled regions of America and plunged into the wilderness as the leaders of the white advance. The Irish Presbyterians were the first and last set of immigrants to do this: all others have merely followed in the wake of their predecessors"

- **President Theodore Roosevelt** in his book "Episodes from the Winning of the West".

General Robert E. Lee, commander of the Confederate Army in the American Civil War, was once asked: "What race do you believe makes the best soldiers?" He replied: "The Scots who came to this country by way of Ireland. Because they have all the dash of the Irish in taking up a position and all the stubbornness of the Scots in holding it".

"Americans are being told in these days that they owe a debt of support to Irish independence because the Irish fought with us in our own struggle for independence. Yes the Irish did and we owe them a debt of support. But it was the Orange Irish who fought in our Revolution and not the Green Irish" - American historian **Owen Wister** in his book "A Straight Deal".

"Call this War by whatever name you may, only call it not an American rebellion: it is nothing more or less than a Scots Irish Presbyterian rebellion" - a **British officer** writing in 1778.

"Presbyterianism is really at the bottom of this whole conspiracy, has supplied it with vigour and will never rest until something is decided upon" - a **representative** of **Lord Dartmouth** writing from New York in 1776.

"Half the Continental Army were from Ireland - Scots Irish" - **British major-general** testifying on the Revolutionary War before a committee of the British House of Commons.

THE FIRST SCOTS-IRISH CONGRESS

In no other American state is the Scots-Irish blood purer than in Tennessee. This was stated at the opening of the first ever congress of the Scotch-Irish Society of America in Columbia, Maury County, middle-Tennessee in May, 1889.

"Among all the states of the Union, none could have been more appropriate for the gathering than Tennessee, both on account of her central geographical position and the blood of her people. Pennsylvania, Maryland, Virginia and North and South Carolina received the first great accessions of Ulster immigration, but swarms from these parent hives, moving westward since colonial days, now make Tennessee the centre of the blood in America" - the opening statement to the Congress declared.

"Besides her immediate position between the extreme North and the extreme South, Tennesseans are freer from sectional prejudice than either of these quarters, and, therefore better fitted to promote the fraternal spirit which the congress was intended to foster.

"Ulster Scots were the earliest and most numerous of Tennessee's pioneers. On the banks of the Watauga, they made the first American settlement west of the Alleghenies, and it was they who led the vanguard in the march of civilisation westward through her territory. They filled the armies that subdued the savages of the West and South West. It was their stern, unalterable courage which prevented Britain and Spain from confining the Americans to the Atlantic slope, and secured the Mississippi valley to the Union.

"Their numbers and valor in every war in which this country has been engaged has won for Tennessee the proud title of 'The Volunteer State'. They stamped their predominant character upon their descendants and gave the prevailing type to the character of the whole people".

The statement continued: "Columbia, the place chosen for the first congress, lies in the very centre of Tennessee and her Scots-Irish population is surrounded by a country widely known as 'the garden spot' of Tennessee. It is a country unsurpassed for salubrity of climate, richness and variety of products, and advantages for geographical position.

"It is not strange that the Scots-Irish should have occupied it first. Always in the foremost ranks of the pioneers, the richest lands became theirs by right of discovery and first occupation, while the poorer country was left to the more timid people, who followed at a later and safer period.

"The advantages thus acquired, and the characteristic tenacity with which they have been held, go far to explain why the race has ever since been the wealthiest and most influential of the people in the countries first settled by them. Among the distinguished men of this stock whom Maury County has produced was James K. Polk, who went from Columbia to the American President's chair".

"

Presbyterian Church order has been described as a democracy run riot. There are so many checks and balances; so much consultation; so many networks of support and defence; so much representation of the periphery at the centre, that it is not easy to get anything changed. Indeed the periphery is so strongly represented at the centre that it is even inappropriate to speak in those terms. Significant change comes about only after maximum information has been provided and extensive debate has taken place at all levels of the Church's life.

There is a deep suspicion of centralised power and a commitment to the concept of accountability. Presbyterian principles influenced the American constitution with its checks and balances and the division of powers between the President, the Congress and the Supreme Court.

"

Rev. Dr. John Dunlop,
Moderator of the Irish Presbyterian Church 1992-93

5

How Tennessee *became a state*

Tennessee became a state of the Union on June 1, 1796. But it took a decade of turmoil in the wake of hostilities in the Ameri can War of Independence before this status was reached.

The cost of the war had left North Carolina virtually bankrupt and with thousands of her people now living west of the Alleghenies there was the problem of lifting land dues and taxes. Mountain settlers like the Wataugans were a fiercely independent breed, nurtured by the dominant Scots-Irish influences. They bluntly refused to heed any tariff directives from a state which had given them absolutely no military protection when they moved west, nor established any form of authority for them in the new lands.

After years of trying to bring the Overmountain people to heel, the North Carolina legislature in April, 1784 ceded the state's western lands to a Confederation Congress. This was the sign that was awaited on the frontier and right away steps were taken to set in motion the embryo of a new state.

A series of meetings at Jonesboro, representative of the three western North Carolina counties - Washington, Sullivan and Greene, authorised the establishment of a new state of Franklin and its first General Assembly met in March, 1785.

The state was named after American statesman Benjamin Franklin; the first governor was John Sevier, the hero of Kings Mountain and the secretary of state was Landon Carter, son of early Watauga pioneer John Carter. Franklin was effectively the successor to the Watauga Association, with the Holston, Watauga and Nolichucky settlements all represented.

North Carolina refused to recognise the new state and successfully blocked its application to the American Continental Congress. For several years confusion reigned with the people of the region facing demands from two state courts, two tax laws and two sets of state officials.

The rule of the new Franklin legislature gradually became untenable and by 1789 it had disappeared completely. George Washington had just become American President and, when North Carolina finally decided to cede its western lands, the region's affairs came under the control of the Continental Congress. This land was referred to as "The Territory of the United States of America South of the River Ohio". It included Kentucky county which was under the control of Virginia until 1792, when Kentucky became a state, and the region that today is Alabama and Mississippi. There was also the area which today roughly coincides with the boundaries of Tennessee.

In 1790, William Blount, another Revolutionary War hero, was appointed by President Washington as Governor of the new territory and as Superintendent of Indian affairs in the South. Blount, settling at Rocky Mount (close to present-day Johnson City) in the Watauga belt, was conciliatory in his dealings with the Cherokee Indians, who felt threatened by the advancement of the frontier, and in this work he was aided by John Sevier and James Robertson, the Watauga leaders.

In 1792, Blount chose the hamlet known as White's Fort as the new capital of the Territory and he commissioned its founder, General James White, of Londonderry stock, to lay out the streets of the town. It was re-named Knoxville after General Henry Knox, Washington's Secretary of War and another Scots-Irish luminary. Blount moved to the town, to live in "Blount's Mansion" close to the Holston River.

The Indian wars were coming to an end and the dialogue over land acquisition and treaties was moving at a rapid pace. The Treaty of Tellico in 1792-93 was conducted between the Territorial Government and the Cherokee chiefs and it brought about a temporary cessation of hostilities. During the last days of the Territorial Government a census of the region was taken and this showed a population of 77,262, of which 10,613 were African slaves. It needed 60,000 for statehood and Daniel Smith, secretary of the Southwest Territory, submitted Tennessee as the name of the new state.

A General Assembly was called in Knoxville in January, 1796 to draw up a state constitution and present were General James Robertson, now of Davidson County, and General John Sevier. Also present was a young Andrew Jackson, a Jonesboro attorney who was now living in Nashville.

The Federal Government accepted Tennessee as the 16th state of the Union, with the state comprising of eight counties in the east and three in the middle. The far western part was still claimed by the Cherokee and Chickasaw Indian tribes. John Sevier was elected Governor; William Blount and Samuel Cocke as the first Senators and Andrew Jackson as the first Congressman. Tennessee had at last achieved statehood, but the bitter disputes over lands with the Indians to the west were far from over.

They were Twain when they crossed the sea,
  And often their folk had warred;
But side by side, on the ramparts wide,
  They cheered as the gates were barred
And they cheered as they passed their King
  To the ford that daunted none,
For field or wall, it was each for all
  When the Lord had made them One.

Thistle and Rose, they twinned them close
  When their fathers crossed the sea,
And they dyed them red, the live and the dead,
  Where the blue starred-lint grows free;
Where the blue starred-lint grows free,
  Here in the Northern sun,
Till His way was plain, He led the Twain,
  And He forged them into One.

They were One when they crossed the sea
  To the land of hope and dream,
Salute them now, whom none could cow,
  Nor hold in light esteem!
Whose footsteps far in peace and war
  Still sought the setting sun!
With a dauntless word and a long bright sword -
  The Twain whom God made One!

W. F. Marshall (Rev),
Co. Tyrone

6

The Wataugans: *the first Tennesseans*

The Watauga Association - widely acknowledged as America's first free and independent community - was founded in North Carolina in May, 1772 by frontier settlers, notable among whom were a significant number of Scots-Irish.

The first settlers of the Watauga and Nolichucky valleys were Virginians who had moved along the Shenandoah valley from Pennsylvania, united in the desire to escape the English colonial domination that was then prevalent in a large part of the Carolinas. These were a hard-working, strong-willed, independent-minded people who, finding little semblance of law or order in the new lands they had moved to, decided to establish their own judicial, and civil system.

Five commissioners were appointed to decide all matters of controversy and to govern and direct for the common good of all the people. Two of the commissioners, cousins James and Charles Robertson, were of direct Scots-Irish descent. The others - John Carter, Zachariah Isbell and Jacob Brown - had English roots.

The Commission settled questions of debt, probated wills, recorded deeds, determined rights of property and issued marriage licences. It also had the ultimate power to hang horse thieves, who were then a scourge in the region. It was a form of authority which lasted six years and was considered by the vast majority of the Overmountain settlers to be an absolute necessity in a wilderness far removed from lawfully appointed government.

The Watauga community was in clear breach of British Government regulations regarding movement by white settlers to lands that were officially designated Cherokee country. Lord Dunmore, the Royal governor of Virginia, reported back to London in 1774 that there were "a set of people in the back part of the colony, bordering on Cherokee country, who finding they could not obtain the land they fancied have set up a separate state".

The Wataugans, however, were undeterred. They were isolated from mainstream authority, outside the jurisdiction of Virginia and geographically separated from the other settlements in North Carolina by forests and mountains.

Under the colonial laws of King George III they were squatters on Indian lands, but finding possession nine-tenths of the law they stubbornly stood their ground and ignored all edicts from Dunmore and the other colonial rulers. The Wataugans set up their own militia and entered into negotiations with the Indians, first to lease the lands from the Cherokees and then to make a permanent purchase. President Theodore Roosevelt, looking back 100 years later, described them as a people who "bid defiance to outsiders".

Tennessee's first permanent settler of record, Captain William Bean, arrived from Virginia in 1768 with his wife Lydia and established a home on the banks of the Watauga River, which was then part of North Carolina. Bean was an associate of the frontier explorer Daniel Boone, which may account for the Boone's Creek name of his Watauga home.

Two years later, James Robertson, arrived after completing the long and arduous journey across the mountains. His stopping-off point was Sycamore Shoals (today in the north eastern tip of Tennessee close to Johnson City) and looking out over the lush Watauga countryside he was convinced that he had at last reached "the promised land".

Robertson was then only 28 and it was the beginning of an illustrious life on America's first western frontier which was to bring him honour as one of the founding fathers, not only of East Tennessee, but Middle Tennessee.

Within a period of two years there were up to 100 farms settled on the banks of the Holston and Watauga Rivers and expansion along the upper reaches was rapid as more and more families poured in, very many of them of Scots-Irish roots. The west side of the Holston River was settled by John Carter (near the site of the present-day town of

Rogersville) and it was to here that the grandparents of Davy Crockett moved. South east of Sycamore Shoals was the Nolichucky River, which flows westward from the Blue Ridge Mountains into the Tennessee-Holston Rivers. The first settlers there were John Ryan and Jacob Brown and both successfully traded with the Cherokee Indian tribes.

The Nolichucky settlement was not originally aligned with the Watauga Association, but as the Revolutionary War progressed they forged close links. The Cherokee Indians who lived in villages south of the Watauga settlements were understandably upset about the existence of these settlements. They expressed worry from time to time in the 1770s, sometimes in words and sometimes in hostile actions.

On one occasion the Indian concern was expressed to Governor Martin, of North Carolina by John Stuart, the superintendent of Indian Affairs : "The Cherokee Nation is still extremely uneasy at the encroachment of the white people on their hunting grounds at Watauga River, where a very large settlement is formed upwards of fifty miles beyond the established boundary, and, as I am apprehensive that it consists of emigrants from your Province to which it is contiguous, I must beg your excellency's interposition to endeavour to prevail on them to remove; otherwise, the serious consequences may in a little time prove very fatal . . . . . . should they then neglect to move off, I am much afraid it will be impossible to restrain the Indians from taking redress themselves by robbing and perhaps murdering some of them."

Despite the threats from Indians and official disapproval by agents of the British government, the Watauga settlers and their neighbours were resolutely determined to develop the area as their permanent home. For the first two years of the Association, the Wataugans lived in relative peace with their lease-holders the Cherokees, but the calm was broken by a few white settlers who still held grudges over earlier Indian attacks on their kinsfolk.

An Indian was shot dead in 1774 while attending sports organised by the white settlers at Sycamore Shoals and, when all the tribesmen returned immediately to their camps, the situation became ominous. James Robertson, however, intervened and with a companion spoke directly to the Cherokee chiefs, expressing regret and offering to make amends for the terrible misdeed of a rogue settler. The Cherokees were pacified, but the war drums of the Shawnee tribes in the upper Ohio River region were beating loudly.

The Shawnee sought an alliance with the Cherokees to hold back the advance of the white man across the Allegheny Mountains: the only solution they saw was war and, under their chief Cornstalk, parted company with the less hostile Cherokees to engage the Overmountain Men at the Battle of Point Pleasant in October, 1774. The Battle of Point Pleasant was a highpoint for the Scots-Irish during the American Revolutionary period. But it could have ended in disaster largely due to the bungling of John Murray, the Earl of Dunmore and Governor of Virginia.

Dunmore, an arrogant Englishman, stands accused by historians of entrapping the Scots-Irish settlers into what would have been inevitable death and annihilation at the hands of the Shawnee Indians had they not been saved by their own determined courage and self-reliance.

General Andrew Lewis had been ordered by Dunmore to assemble the men of Kentucky and western Virginia, together with those from the Overmountain stations in what today is East Tennessee and North Carolina, and to proceed to the "Point" at the junction of the Ohio and Kanawha Rivers. There, they were to link up with Dunmore and his army and march against the Indians who were gathering in great force along the western frontier.

Twelve hundred men answered the call, with a force of Wataugans led by James Robertson, Isaac Shelby and John Sevier. The journey of several hundred miles took them dangerously into unknown forests and mountain regions and when the "Point" was eventually reached in October, 1774, neither Dunmore, nor his army, were to be seen. Their journey had been delayed.

A camp was set up, as Dunmore's arrival was awaited, but James Robertson, a soldier with strong Ulster blood in his veins, became restless and uneasy with the suspense of waiting. Rising in the early dawn, he decided, with a comrade, to check out the position on the outer reaches of the camp. They had hardly walked for more than a mile when they heard stirrings in the undergrowth. There, just a few hundred yards away, were bands of Indians, ready to attack. Realising the danger, Robertson and his comrade raced back to the camp and roused the sleeping men with the dreaded frontier cry of "Indians". Long rifles were cocked in readiness for the Indians advancing on the encampment they had intended to take by surprise.

The battle raged for most of October 10, 1774, with heavy casualties sustained on both sides in the rifle fire and hand-to-hand combat. The Indians were also armed with rifles, urged on by their chief Cornstalk with the words "Be strong, be strong". As night approached General Lewis assigned Isaac Shelby and his Overmountainmen to break up Cornstalk's rear and he himself made a simultaneous attack from the front. These tactics worked. The Indians were forced into a wild panic and fled back to their canoes on the Ohio River, leaving their dead and injured behind.

Dunmore, on hearing of the battle Lewis and his men had been forced into, ordered the troops to disband and return home. But Lewis was not in the mood for obeying any more orders from this gentleman and he and his men marched on Dunmore at Charlotte where a confrontation took place. One account recalls: "A furious scene followed, and if Lewis had not restrained his men, they would have put Dunmore to death".

The Battle of Point Pleasant made possible the Treaty of Charlotte by which the Indians were finally excluded from Virginia. Lord Dunmore's War between the frontier militias and the Shawnee Indians was said to be provoked by Scots-Irish frontiersmen, waged by Scots-Irish frontiersmen and won by Scots-Irish frontiersmen. It was the first war on the western frontier and it secured both the settlement of Kentucky and opened up more pathways across the Allegheny Mountains to the west.

When the Watauga Association was set up in 1772 mainly by Scots-Irish settlers in the region that today is in East Tennessee, Lord Dunmore blasted the development as "a dangerous example". He pointed out : "It is an encouragement to the people of America of forming governments distinct from and independent of His Majesty's authority," he said.

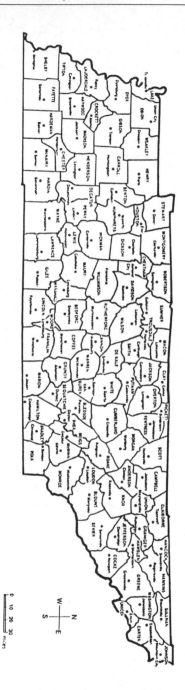

TENNESSEE: Counties and County Seats

7

Turning Point *at Kings Mountain*

T he unrelenting Scots-Irish character was never more evident on the American frontier than at the Battle of Kings Mountain on October 7, 1780. The British suffered such a catastrophic setback on this South Carolina battlefield that its rule on the American colonies effectively came to an end and independence was reinforced for the fledgling nation.

Those mainly responsible were the Scots-Irish Presbyterians who had fled their native lands for the new frontier world to acquire freedom to live and worship as they pleased. It was they, more than any other of the nationalities involved, who halted the British in their tracks at Kings Mountain and secured victory in the Revolutionary War.

The American quest for independence was settled at Kings Mountain by a determined band of militiamen recruited among the humble frontier farmlands of the Scots-Irish, English, German and Dutch and French Huguenot settlers. After Kings Mountain loyalist fervour for the Crown dissipated and the frontiers were pushed back in the expansion towards the American independence dream.

One of the ironies of the Kings Mountain engagement was that all but one of the participants was American. There were patriot volunteers on the side of independence against loyalists who favoured the continuation of British rule in the colonies. The one notable exception was a Scot, Colonel Patrick Ferguson, an Aberdonian attached to His Majesty's 71st Highlanders. As the leading soldier in the British Army of the day, Ferguson was drafted in to lead a force of American loyalists to quell the rebellion and it was an action that was to tragically cost him his life.

The loyalists who backed the Crown at Kings Mountain came from a variety of backgrounds. Many were highland Scots, like Ferguson, and some were English settlers with strong Tory and Anglican roots. They came largely from North Carolina, and New York, the most loyalist of the American states during the Revolutionary War, but a state which paradoxically was the first to vote for independence.

Patrick Ferguson, the inventor of the first breechloading rifle used in the British Army, served under the command of Lord Cornwallis at Charleston and as Inspector of the Militia in the Southern Provinces he raised a loyalist militia force of some 4,000.

Both sides in the American dispute violently harassed one another, with attacks being carried out by both the loyalist factions and the revolutionary groups. Throughout the summer and autumn of 1780 these continued with ferocity.

It was the western region, across the Blue Ridge Mountains, which was causing Ferguson most worry and he sent a message to the Overmountain men to "desist from their opposition to the British arms, and take protection under his standard". If they did not Ferguson threatened to "march the loyalist army over the mountain, hang their leaders and lay their country waste with fire and sword".

The message had the opposite effect: the Overmountain men began preparing for anything which Ferguson saw fit to throw at him, their resolve was to maintain their cultural identity and their independence. The resistance was led by French Huguenot John Sevier, Welshman Isaac Shelby, and William Campbell and Charles McDowell, two men of Scots-Irish families from Virginia and North Carolina.

The big problem facing the Overmountain men, however, was finance - the money to fully equip a militia strong enough to take on Ferguson and his loyalists. John Sevier tried personally to raise funds, but found that the settlers had mortgaged themselves heavily on their lands and there was simply no money to spare. The mainland entry taker to North Carolina John Adair had just taken possession of their money and it was to him that Sevier and Isaac Shelby eventually turned.

Adair, born in Co. Antrim near the present-day Ulster town of Ballymena, was a patriot sympathiser, a solid Presbyterian. He did not need much persuading to hand over the money to be used in the cause of independence. His immortal words summed up the attitude of people of his kinsfolk on the American frontier at the time: "Colonel Sevier, I have no authority by law to make this disposition of the money. It belongs to the impoverished treasury of North Carolina and I dare not appropriate a cent of it to any purpose. But if the country is over-run by the British, their liberty is gone. Take it, if the enemy, by its use, is driven from this country, I can trust that country to justify and vindicate my conduct. So take it".

Both Sevier and Shelby personally pledged to repay the 12,735 dollars received from Adair. The Overmountain men were armed and prepared to face the onslaught from Ferguson and his loyalists at Kings Mountain.

The call to arms spread like wildfire among the mountain people and on September 25, on the flats at Sycamore Shoals, the territory that today encapsulates the town of Elizabethton close to Johnson City in North East Tennessee, a large gathering of settlers, in excess of 1,000, assembled.

Few of these combatants had the appearance of soldiers going into battle; they were small dirt farmers who had just left their lands, garbed in rough mountain-style clothes and carrying the barest of utensils. The most effective weapon each shouldered was the Kentucky long rifle, the traditional firepower of the American frontier. John Sevier commanded 240 men from Washington County (then North Carolina now Tennessee); Isaac Shelby a similar force from nearby Sullivan County; William Campbell led 400 Virginians and Charles McDowell 160 from South Carolina. More were to join from South Carolina.

The womenfolk also gathered at Sycamore Shoals to bid their farewells and to ensure that the volunteers had enough food and clothing for the assignment. And there was the Rev. Samuel Doak ..... his presence was significant in bringing spiritual guidance to those preparing for battle.

Doak, a Scots-Irish Presbyterian minister in the best traditions of the 18th century Calvinism, likened the cause of the Overmountain settlers to that of Gideon and his people in opposing the Midianites in Biblical times. "The Sword of the Lord and Gideon" he offered as the battle cry, with the assembled gathering loudly echoing his words before starting off on horseback on the long journey to face Ferguson and the loyalists. An overall leader was required and after consultation between Sevier, Shelby and McDowell, William Campbell, the six foot, six inches giant of Ulster vintage, was chosen. He was a Virginian, the other officers were from North Carolina.

It took 10 days before the patriot force came in sight of Ferguson's army: the distinctive red uniforms of the loyalists standing out in the rugged mountain terrain. Campbell's men dug into the wooded areas, while Ferguson decided on an open ridge for his base. After reviewing the platoons under his command, Campbell advised anyone who did not wish to fight to head for home immediately. There were no takers and after he ordered them to "shout like hell and fight like devils" his men responded to the first fire mounted from the Tory ranks.

The battle lasted 65 minutes, the revolutionary forces using Indian-style tactics to out-manoeuvre the loyalists from the back of every tree, rock and shrub. There was much hand-to-hand fighting and the prowess of the long riflemen gradually took its toll. The Redcoats were forced to defend their position with bayonets as the Overmountain men closed in. Colonel Ferguson, probably sensing defeat, had to personally ward off attacks from all sides. A rifle shot struck him in the head and slumping in the saddle he dropped from his horse, dead. His command was taken by Captain Abraham DePeyster, who had engaged the mountainmen in a previous battle at Musgrove's Mill.

It was a hopeless cause. The loyalists were encircled and in panic some waved white flags of surrender. But the shooting continued, with many of the patriots unaware of the significance of the white flags.

They were not professional soldiers and the revenge factor surfaced as previous atrocities committed by loyalists came to mind. Eventually, Colonel Campbell managed to bring about a ceasefire among his ranks by calling out: "For God's sake, don't shoot. It is murder to kill them now, for they have raised their flags". DePeyster protested at the behaviour of the patriots: "It's damned unfair, damned unfair". Campbell calmly ignored the protestations, calling on loyalists to sit down as "prisoners".

The Overmountain men had fairly minimal casualties compared to the loyalists: 28 killed and 62 wounded against 225 dead; 163 wounded and about 800 taken prisoner.

Kings Mountain was the watershed in the Revolutionary War, the left flank of Lord Cornwallis had been effectively shattered and the British were never again able to muster a loyalist force of size from

American society. Patrick Ferguson was buried close to the ridge he had chosen to defend. He was just 36 when he died, a soldier whose bravery and technical military skills were as much admired by those whom he fought as those who had served under him.

A letter written by Patrick Ferguson to his mother early in his American service gives an indication of the type of God-fearing man he was. It read: "The length of our lives is not at our command, however much the manner of them may be. If our Creator enables us to act the part of honour and to conduct ourselves with spirit, probity and humanity, the change to another world whether now or in 50 years hence, will not be for the worse".

The loyalist prisoners were taken to Hillsborough, North Carolina, where they were exchanged for patriot prisoners. Most of the Overmountain men drifted back to their farms and their families - their involvement in the war was over. It took a week for news of the Kings Mountain defeat to reach Cornwallis and it had a devastating effect. Plans for an offensive in the south west were abandoned although British authorities in New York tried to dismiss the Battle result as of no consequence.

General George Washington did not hear of the Kings Mountain battle until October 26, and, with elation, he spoke of "that important object gained" as "proof of the spirit and resources of the country". In later years, Thomas Jefferson was to recall "that memorable victory" at Kings Mountain "the joyful annunciation of that turn of the tide of success which terminated the Revolutionary War with the seal of independence".

The leaders of the patriot forces in the Battle became leading politicians and civic leaders. John Sevier was the first Governor of Tennessee; Isaac Shelby the first Governor of Kentucky, while William Campbell represented Washington County in the Virginia House of Delegates before an untimely death 10 months after Kings Mountain. Many others were to distinguish themselves in politics and in subsequent army careers, but most went back to being simple farmers.

MARY PATTON THE POWDER MAKER

An English woman of Scottish parentage married to an Ulsterman was one of the heroines of the American Revolutionary War - she made the black gunpowder that was vital to the success of the revolutionaries.

Mary McKeehan had been shown the art of gunpowder making as a child in England by her father David, before the family emigrated to Pennsylvania in the late 1760s. At about the same time John Patton stole passage on a ship headed from the north of Ireland to America. He was of Scots-Irish Presbyterian stock, having been born in Ulster in 1749.

John settled in Carlisle, Pennsylvania and in the early years of the Revolution served in the local militia. Mary McKeehan and he married in 1772 and they set up a powder-making operation in the Cumberland County region of Pennsylvania.

They had two young children and, finding Pennsylvania being overrun by Redcoats, they sold their business and headed to the Sycamore Shoals / Elizabethton / Johnson City area of North Carolina which today is in East Tennessee.

There, they were assisted in establishing a gunpowder mill by Andrew Taylor, another Scots-Irish settler who fought with John in the Pennsylvania militia.

Mary was the one most proficient in powder making and the simple instrument she used was a large black kettle. For the Battle of Kings Mountain on October 7, 1780 she made 500 pounds of black gunpowder for the Overmountain Men, a revolutionary force consisting mostly of Scots-Irish settlers. This potent mix was an essential ingredient in ensuring victory for the Overmountain Men against the 1,100-strong British force, commanded by Colonel Patrick Ferguson. It was the turning point of the Revolutionary War.

Mary Patton did not receive national acclaim for the part she played in the Revolutionary War, but in East Tennessee and North Carolina she is still looked upon as a woman of great courage and heroism.

Mary taught other members of her family to manufacture gunpowder and the Patton mill continued in production for upwards of 100 years. It was in use during the Civil War. The processes involved in the manufacture of black powder were the production of saltpeter and charcoal and in the cottage industry operation of the Patton mill much hand labour was required. The powder was packed in 25, 50 and 100 pound kegs.

ULSTER-BORN VETERANS OF KINGS MOUNTAIN

The Battle of Kings Mountain in South Carolina on October 7, 1780 is widely acknowledged by historians as the turning point of the American Revolutionary War. The Overmountain Men, numbering about 1,400 mostly of Scots-Irish origin, decisively defeated the British force of 1,100 Redcoat soldiers under Colonel Patrick Ferguson in an hour-long battle.

Ferguson and 225 of his men were killed; 163 were wounded and the rest were captured. Only 28 of the mountain men were killed and 62 wounded. Most of the Scots-Irish riflemen who fought at Kings Mountain were first, second or third generation Americans of Ulster-born parents or grandparents. But a good many were born in Ireland, a few in the South, but the overwhelming number in the North of the island and from the Presbyterian tradition of Scots-Irish.

Known Irish-born Kings Mountaineers were:

Joseph Alexander: Born Co. Antrim, May 1759. Joseph entered service in 1775 while residing in Spartanburg, South Carolina. Before Kings Mountain he fought at the battles of Musgrove's Mill and Blackstock's Plantation. He acted as a scout on the Indian frontier and was made a lieutenant in 1781. Joseph finally settled at Clermont County, Ohio.

William Armstrong: Born north of Ireland, August 1765. William volunteered while residing in Fairfield, South Carolina and before Kings Mountain was at the battles of Rocky Mountain, Bratton's Plantation, Hanging Rock and Fishing Creek. After Kings Mountain, he fought the British at Eutaw Springs and was at Cowpens when the Redcoats left.

Alexander Bailey: Born north of Ireland, 1751. Alexander enlisted in 1776 in Rowan County, North Carolina and served on several expeditions to fight the Indians. He was involved in the various South Carolina skirmishes and joined with the Wataugans in the march across the Blue Ridge to Kings Mountain. He died in Sullivan County, Indiana in 1835.

Andrew Bigham: Born north of Ireland, August 1760. Andrew was a resident of Mecklenburg County, North Carolina when he entered service in 1779. He served at Kings Mountain in the Third Regiment of Militia. He finally settled in McMinn County, Tennessee.

John Boyce: Born north of Ireland, about 1740. John, a Newberry, South Carolina settler, was wounded in the attempt to storm Savannah. Apart from Kings Mountain, he also fought the British at Blackstock's Plantation, Cowpens, and Eutaw Springs. He died in South Carolina in 1806.

Gerard Brandon: Born Co. Donegal. Aligned himself with the cause of Robert Emmet in Ireland before moving to Charleston in South Carolina. He led a cavalry charge at Kings Mountain and also fought at Cowpens. He eventually settled in Mississippi where his son G.C. Brandon was twice governor.

Captain John Brown: Born Londonderry, 1738. John Brown emigrated to Lancaster County, Pennsylvania in 1763 and was a school teacher. By 1770 he had moved to North Carolina and served in the local militia, first as an ensign and then as second lieutenant. He led a company at Kings Mountain and was among the first magistrates and state legislators when Wilkes County was formed in North Carolina.

William Caldwell: Born near Belfast, 1760. William was brought to America by his parents and it was while resident in Spartanburg district, South Carolina in 1780 that he enlisted. At Kings Mountain he saved the life of a comrade by removing a bayonet that pinned the man's hand to his thigh. He also served at Cowpens and died in 1840.

Major William Candler: Born Belfast, 1736. Another who was taken to America as a child, William lived with his family in Virginia and after working as a surveyor he saw army service at Augusta, Siege of Savannah, Kings Mountain and Blackstock's Plantation. At Kings Mountain he commanded a Georgia Militia Unit. He rose to the rank of Colonel and died in 1789 in Richland (Columbia) County, Georgia.

Captain Patrick Carr: Born Co. Londonderry about 1740. He settled in Georgia before the Revolutionary War and apart from Kings Mountain he served at Blackstock's Plantation. He was promoted to

Major and fought the Tories and Indians in Georgia. It is claimed he killed 100 Tories by his own hand during the war. He was murdered possibly by a descendant of a Tory at Jefferson County, Geogia in 1802.

Samuel Clowney (Cluney): Born north of Ireland, 1743. Samuel was an express rider, militia man and powder maker at the various battles - Reedy River, Kings Mountain, Blackstock's Plantation and Cowpens. Settled in Union District, South Carolina about 1775 and died there in 1824.

John Copeland: Born north of Ireland, 1760. John left Ireland as a 14-year-old, settling with his father in York District, South Carolina. In the Revolutionary War he served first as a private, then as a lieutenant. he fought the Cherokees and at Kings Mountain he remained behind to erect structures to shelter the wounded.

Major Joseph Dickson: Born north of Ireland, 1745. Joseph settled in Rowan County, North Carolina and became a captain early in the Revolutionary War. As a major he commanded the south fork men at Kings Mountain and in 1781 he was promoted to the rank of colonel. He served in the South Carolina state senate, was a member of Congress and a general in the militia. He was also a prominent Mason and in 1806 moved to Rutherford County, Tennessee. He died there in 1825.

Captain James Dysart: Born Co. Donegal, 1744. James Dysart's parents died when he was an infant and he was raised by his grandfather. In 1761 he landed in Philadelphia and settled in the Holston Valley which today is in East Tennessee. He was involved in early exploration of Tennessee and Kentucky. As a captain at Kings Mountain, he received a serious hand wound. He became a major and colonel in latter affrays in the war and represented Washington County in the Tennessee legislature. He died at Rockcastle County, Kentucky in 1818.

Arthur Erwin: Born Co. Antrim, 1738. Arthur, son of Nathaniel Erwin, came to America with his parents and settled in Bucks County, Pennsylvania. While in settlement at Catawba River in North Carolina he enlisted and served at Kings Mountain.

Bellingsby Gibson: Born near Londonderry, 1750. Bellingsby landed in America in 1775 and settled at Lancaster County, Pennsylvania. He moved to Rockbridge County, Virginia and enlisted in the militia. He served at Valley Forge, Sandy Hook and Kings Mountain. Was living in Washington County in Tennessee in 1832.

Colonel James Hawthorn: Born Co. Armagh, Ireland, 1750. James settled on the frontier of South Carolina and was captured for a time by Indians along with his mother and two sisters about 1762. He became a blacksmith in York County and served under Colonel Thomas Neel, his father-in-law, in the Snow Campaign of 1775. He fought the Cherokees in 1776 and was a first lieutenant in the 6th South Carolina Regiment. In the Florida Expedition he was a captain and rose in rank to adjutant, major and lieutenant colonel. At Kings Mountain he was in charge of a battalion and at Cowpens he was wounded. He died at Livingston County, Kentucky in 1809.

Colonel William Hill: Born Belfast, 1740. While serving as a colonel in the South Carolina militia William Hill was in the battle of Rocky Mount and Hanging Rock, before moving to Kings Mountain and Cowpens. He died in 1816.

Captain James Johnson: Born north of Ireland about 1755. James served as a private, lieutenant, captain and adjutant with the South Carolina militia in all the main battles of the war.

David Kirkwood: Born Dunbean, north of Ireland, 1740. While residing in Pittsburg David Kirkwood enlisted and was in engagements against the British at Stoney Point, Long Island, Trenton, Princeton, and Brandywine. About 1780, he moved south and joined the Wataugans at Kings Mountain. After the war he moved to Champaign, Ohio and died in 1847.

James Laird: Born north of Ireland 1735. James, of Washington County, Virginia, served as an ensign under Colonel William Campbell at Kings Mountain. He settled in Sullivan County, Tennessee and died in Grainger County, Tennessee in 1826.

John Long: Born Londonderry, 1737. John Long served under the command of Colonel Isaac Shelby at the battle of Kings Mountain. He settled in Sullivan County, Tennessee and died in Grainger County, Tennessee in 1826.

Samuel Mackie: Born Co. Tyrone, Ireland, 1761. Samuel first entered service as a volunteer militiaman in Burke County, North Carolina in February, 1780. He was a dragoon in the mounted militia, served for a while with the South Carolina forces and at Kings Mountain fought under Colonels Campbell, Shelby and Sevier. He died in Franklin County, Georgia in 1845.

Michael Mahoney: Michael was born in the south of Ireland and settled on the Nollichucky River in what today is East Tennessee. He was killed at Kings Mountain while serving under Colonel John Sevier.

Captain Samuel Martin: Born Co. Tyrone 1732. After arriving in America Samuel moved from Pennsylvania to Tryon County, North Carolina. He engaged in the numerous battles with the Indians and at Kings Mountain six of his 20-man company were killed. He died, aged 96, in Lincoln County, North Carolina.

Captain Edward Martin: Born north of Ireland, 1758. Edward enlisted as a private while in settlement at Fairfield, North Carolina. He became a captain, serving at Kings Mountain. He died in 1813.

Lieutenant-Colonel Charles McLean: Born north of Ireland, 1726. Charles emigrated to America with his brother Ephraim and, while settled in Tryon County, North Carolina, he served as a major and a lieutenant colonel in the Second Battalion North Carolina Militia. He and Ephraim served at Kings Mountain. A son Ephraim was the first ordained minister of the Cumberland Presbyterian Church. Charles died in Logan County, Kentucky in 1805.

Captain Ephraim McLean: Born Ulster (Northern Ireland), 1730. A brother of Charles, Ephraim received his commission as a captain at Tryon County, North Carolina and served at Kings Mountain. After the war he represented Burke County in the North Carolina senate. He died in Greenvale, Kentucky.

William McMaster: Born North of Ireland 1759. William came to America with his parents at the age of 13. He enlisted while resident at Savannah River, South Carolina and served in all the main battles. He was wounded in action.

David Miller: Born north of Ireland, 1725. David Miller, his wife and five children sailed from Ireland to America about 1760-64 and settled in Old Tryon (now Rutherford County), North Carolina, where he accumulated 30,000 acres of land. He was appointed land entry-taker for Rutherford County in 1779 and sat in the North Carolina assembly. He was surveyor and during service in the South Carolina Militia he acted as chaplain to the unit and was at Kings Mountain. When called upon to pray at a Presbyterian Church meeting at the time Miller proceeded as follows: "Good Lord, our God in Heaven, we have good reason to thank Thee for the many favours we have received at Thy hands, the many battles we have won: there is the great and glorious battle of Kings Mountain, where we kilt the great Gineral Ferguson and took his whole army, and the great battles at Ramsour's and at Williamson's, and the ever-memorable and glorious battle of the Coopens, where we made the proud Gineral Tarleton run doon the road helter-skelter, and good Lord, if ya na have suffered the cruel Tories to burn Billy Hill's ironworks, we would na have asked any mair favors at Thy hands. Amen." * Sic.

Captain James Miller: Born north of Ireland, 1730. James Miller commanded a company of the North Carolina militia at Kings Mountain. He became a colonel a year later and led troops in the expedition against the Cherokee Indians. He served as a state senate in South Carolina and died in 1812.

John Miller: Born north of Ireland, 1737. "Hopping John" was a ranger and a sergeant in the South Carolina Militia, before becoming adjutant. He served at Kings Mountain, Blackstock's Plantation, and Eutaw Springs, ending up as a lieutenant.

David Morton: Born north of Ireland, 1761. David enlisted in the militia while living in Spartanburg, South Carolina. He was at the battles of Kings Mountain and Blackstock's Plantation, and at Cowpens.

Patrick Murphy: Born Co. Kerry, Ireland. Patrick resided in Washington County, North Carolina and was wounded while serving under Colonel John Sevier at Kings Mountain.

Walter O'Neill: Born Co. Wexford, Ireland, 1760. Walter was a volunteer militiaman in Burke County, North Carolina and fought at the various battles in the region, including Kings Mountain, Ramsour's Mill, and Cowpens. He finished his service guarding the frontier against the Cherokee Indians. He was living in Fayette County, Pennsylvania in 1833.

Arthur Patterson: Born north of Ireland. Arthur resided at Kings Creek in North Carolina near the Kings Mountain battlefield. He took an active role in the battle and three of his sons Arthur Jun., Thomas and William were taken prisoner.

John Patterson: Born north of Ireland, 1763. John enlisted in the militia as a substitute for his father Samuel in 1778 and saw action against the Indians. He fought at Kings Mountain and was a light horseman in the hostilities in Virginia. He ended guarding the fords of the Catawba River. By 1832, he was living in Preble County, Ohio.

John Rhea: Born Londonderry, 1753, John, the son of the Rev. Joseph Rhea (1715-77), emigrated to Pennsylvania in 1769, to Maryland in 1771 and to the North Carolina frontier in 1778. He served as a colour bearer at Kings Mountain and as a politician held offices as Sullivan County clerk, member of the North Carolina House of Commons, delegate to the convention which drafted Tennessee's first constitution and a member of the Tennessee House of Representatives. He was in the United States House of Representatives for 18 years. He died in 1832.

George Rutledge: Born Co. Tyrone, 1755. George settled at Sullivan County in North Carolina (in what today is East Tennessee) and served at Kings Mountain under Colonel Isaac Shelby. He was a member of the first Tennessee legislature and a senator in the third. He rose to the rank of brigadier general in the Militia and a county in Tennessee was named in his honour. He died in Blountsville, Tennessee in 1813.

John Scott: Born Co. Antrim, 1754. John emigrated to Charleston in 1770 with his family and settled at Williamsburg in South Carolina. He became a lieutenant in the Militia and apart from Kings Mountain saw action at the siege of Savannah, Black Mingow and Eutaw Springs. By 1841 he was residing at White County, Illinois.

Robert Shannon: Born north of Ireland, 1753. Robert, of Lincoln County, North Carolina, was involved throughout the entire Revolutionary War and at Kings Mountain he held the rank of lieutenant. He died in Henry County, Kentucky in 1827.

Lieutenant Colonel James Steen: Born Co. Antrim, 1734. This sturdy Ulsterman had been involved in the battles with the Indians before the Revolutionary War began and led a company in the Snow Campaign in 1776. He was at Charleston, the siege of Savannah and in the battles of Rocky Mountain, Hanging Rock, Musgrove's Mill, Kings Mountain and Cowpens. In the summer of 1781 he was stabbed to death while attempting to arrest a Tory in Rowan County, North Carolina.

Captain Samuel Ware: Born north of Ireland, 1750. Samuel was a captain in the Virginia militia in 1775 and with his brother John battled with the Indians. He was also a captain under Colonel John Sevier at Kings Mountain. He became involved in politics and was a member of the convention which drew up the constitution of Tennessee. For many years he was clerk of Sevier County in Tennessee and was a major in the Creek War of 1812. His first wife Mary Polly (Lyle) Thompson was born in Co. Antrim in 1757 and died in Tennessee in 1797.

William White: Born north of Ireland, 1773. William joined the South Carolina Militia and after serving at Kings Mountain and other battles he guarded Tory prisoners at Orangeburg.

William Wosson (Wasson): Born Co. Antrim, about 1750. William emigrated to Pennsylvania in 1775 and had service at Princeton with a local militia. After moving to Virginia he continued his revolutionary zeal and fought at Kings Mountain. By 1832 he was living at Greenfield, Gallia County, Ohio.

SONS OF IRISH PARENTS

Samuel Morrow: Was born of Ulster-born parents at Baltimore in Maryland in 1760 just after the family had arrived from Ireland. The family lived at Spartanburg, South Carolina and Samuel enlisted as a 16-year-old. He held the rank of corporal, serving at the various battles, including Kings Mountain. His wife Janet Nelson was born in Co. Down in 1760 and was brought to America by her parents in 1772.

Kings Mountain patriots **Josiah, Robert** and **Samuel Culbertson** were of the family from Ballygan outside Ballymoney in Co. Antrim. The Culbertsons, after emigrating from Ulster in the 1750s, moved down the Great Wagon Road to South Carolina. Samuel was a captain in the militia.

Brothers **James** and **Robert Porter** were born in Pennsylvania of Irish parents. Major James lived at Rutherford County, North Carolina and Greenville County, South Carolina. William, after the war, served in the North Carolina legislature.

The parents of **Joseph Brown Jun.**, were both born in Ulster and lived in Guildford, North Carolina. Joseph enlisted in the militia when only 16 and was 20 when the battle of Kings Mountain was fought. He also went on expeditions against the Indians.

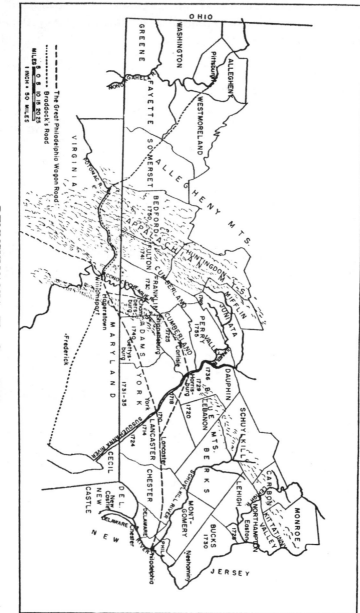

PENNSYLVANIA: The Great Valley

8

The Scots-Irish *Presidents*

Eleven of the 41 Presidents of the United States can definitely trace their direct ancestry back to the Scots-Irish: three (Andrew Jackson, James Buchanan and Chester Alan Arthur) came from first generation parents. Three - Andrew Jackson, James Knox Polk and Andrew Johnson were Tennesseans.

• **Andrew Jackson:** (Democrat - 7th President 1829-37). Born on March 15, 1767 in the Waxhaw region of North Carolina, his family had left Ulster in 1765, having lived in the village of Boneybefore near Carrickfergus. Andrew helped draft the constitution for Tennessee, which became the 16th state of the Union on June 1, 1796.

• **James K. Polk:** (Democrat - 11th President 1845-49). Born on November 2, 1795 near Charlotte in North Carolina, he is descended from a Robert Polk (Pollok) of Londonderry, who had arrived in the American colonies about 1680. Was a Governor of Tennessee and he and his wife Sarah are buried in the State Capital in Nashville.

• **James Buchanan:** (Democrat - 15th President 1857-61). Born on April 23, 1791 in Mercersburg, Pennsylvania, he was born into a Presbyterian home like his predecessors Jackson and Polk. The family came originally from Deroran near Omagh and left Donegal for America in 1783.

• **Andrew Johnson:** (Democrat - 17th President 1865-69). Born on December 29, 1808 in Raleigh, North Carolina, his namesake and grandfather from Mounthill outside Larne had come to America about 1750, from Larne, Co. Antrim. He rose to the Presidency from humble log cabin origins and worked as a tailor for many years.

• **Ulysses Simpson Grant:** (Republican - 18th President 1869-77). The man who commanded the Union Army in the American Civil War, his mother Hannah Simpson was descended from the Simpson family of Dergenagh near Dungannon. His great grandfather John Simpson had left Ulster for America in 1760.

• **Chester Alan Arthur:** (Republican - 21st president 1881-85). Born on October 5, 1830 in Fairfield, Vermont, his grandfather and father, Baptist pastor William Arthur, emigrated to the United States from Dreen near Cullybackey in Co. Antrim in 1801.

• **Grover Cleveland:** (Democrat - 22nd and 24th President 1885-89 and 1893-97). Born on March 18, 1837 in Caldwell, New Jersey, his maternal grandfather Abner Neal had left Co. Antrim in the late 18th century. Son of a Presbyterian minister.

• **Benjamin Harrison:** (Republican - 23rd President 1889-93). Born on August 20, 1833 at North Bend, Ohio, two of his great grandfathers James Irwin and William McDowell were Ulstermen.

• **William McKinley:** (Republican - 25th President 1897-1901). Born on January 29, 1843 in Niles, Ohio, he was the great grandson of James McKinley, who had emigrated to America from Conagher, near Ballymoney in Co. Antrim about 1743.

• **Woodrow Wilson:** (Democrat - 28th President 1913-21). Born December 28, 1856 in Staunton, Virginia, he was the grandson of James Wilson, who had emigrated to North Carolina from Dergalt, Co. Tyrone about 1807. His father Dr. Joseph Ruggles Wilson was a Presbyterian minister.

• **Richard Millhouse Nixon:** (Republican - 37th President 1969-74). Born on January 13, 1913 in Yorba Linda, California, he has Ulster connections on two sides of his family. His Nixon ancester left Co. Antrim for America around 1753, while the Millhouses came from Carrickfergus and Ballymoney. He died in 1994.

TENNESSEANS IN THE WHITE HOUSE

ANDREW JACKSON

A few feet from the shores of Belfast Lough at Carrickfergus stands a plaque which marks the humble birthplace of one of the founding fathers of the state of Tennessee. Andrew Jackson, the seventh President of the United States, was the son of linen weavers who left the North of Ireland in 1765 to seek a better life in the new lands of the Americas.

Jackson, lawyer, soldier and politician of distinction - was the first American President to rise from a log cabin home in the frontier and his colourful career is the embodiment of the opportunity ideal which has long been a central core of life in the United States. The first six American Presidents came from very solid financial backgrounds, of upper and middle class pedigrees.

Orphaned at an early age, Jackson made his mind up quickly that he would strive to reach the highest station in life. His formative education was basic, but he had a good brain, could be quite eloquent when meeting more highly-placed people and he had ambition, loads of it.

His parents Andrew and Elizabeth Jackson (nee Hutchinson) lived for a few years of their marriage in the tiny Co. Antrim hamlet of Boneybefore, about one mile from the town of Carrickfergus. They were descended from lowland Scottish Presbyterians who moved to the northern part of Ireland (the Province of Ulster) about 1639 from the Wigtonshire region and settled in Counties Antrim, Londonderry and Down.

Two forebears of Andrew and Elizabeth - John and Peter Jackson - were made freemen of Carrickfergus in 1683, just seven years before King William III (The Prince of Orange) arrived at the port with his army to prepare for battle with King James II at the Boyne - a battle which was arguably the most significant event in Irish history.

Linen weaving was the trade of many of those who held small holdings in Ulster in the mid-18th century - it had been introduced to the region a century before by the French Huguenot Protestants - and at Boneybefore the Jackson family would have had a reasonable existence for the time, but could in no way be described as affluent.

It was a period of large movement from the north of Ireland to the new lands in America and in the 1760-1770 decade an estimated 21,000 people emigrated from the main ports of Belfast, Larne, Newry, Londonderry and Portrush in a total of 149 vessels. Over a 100-year period until the early 19th century it is estimated that no fewer than 250,000 emigrated.

Andrew and Elizabeth Jackson, with sons Hugh and Robert, made the 12-mile journey to the port of Larne where they set sail for Charleston in South Carolina. Within a short time of arrival they had acquired 200 acres of frontier farm lands at Waxhaw settlement in South Carolina and young Andrew was born on March 15, 1767, a few weeks after the death of his father.

There are those who would dispute that Andrew Jackson was born in America - a requirement at the time for every major political office in the country. One claim is that he was born at sea while his parents were on their way across from Ireland, but reliable historians today give this little credence.

The loss of her husband and the prospect of rearing three children in the harsh wilderness of the Carolinas played long on the mind of Elizabeth Jackson and she took refuge with her sister Jane Crawford, who had also settled in the region at the same time with her husband James and family.

Growing up in the restless, turbulent world of the frontier lands fortified Andrew Jackson with an independent streak and the self-assurance that he was to need when making his way in the law, in the army and in politics. His two brothers died during the Revolutionary War with the British - Hugh from injuries received in battle and Robert from smallpox. His mother had gone to Charleston to meet a couple of nephews who were on a British prison ship in the harbour and she contracted the ship's fever while there and died before she could return home.

These deaths had a devastating effect on young Andrew, alone in the world at the age of 14, and they reinforced his deeply-held hatred of the British. This hostility first emerged in 1779 when Andrew was taken prisoner as a 12-year-old by British forces, along with his brother Robert. The British had wrecked the house they were held captive in and an officer ordered Andrew to clean his boots. When he refused the officer struck him in the face with a sabre, cutting his upraised hand to the bone and leaving a scar on his head that he carried for life.

The years immediately after the deaths of his mother and brothers brought the red-headed, hot tempered Andrew Jackson on to the wild side of life in the Carolinas and with his reckless streak he became involved in many tavern brawls, squaring up to men twice his age and build. He was then hired to the saddlery trade.

He managed to squander a small inheritance from his mother's family back in Ireland as he pursued his over-indulgence for gambling at horse racing, card playing and cock fights. The company he was keeping as a teenager living in Salisbury, North Carolina was not good and his reputation as a rowdy went ahead of him.

However, for all his rebelliousness, Jackson managed to find the time to study law and in 1787 at the age of 20 he was proficient enough to be admitted to the North Carolina bar. He became public prosecutor of North Carolina's western district and, within a year he had crossed the Allegheny mountains into territory that was to become in 1796 the state of Tennessee. There he set up a law office in Nashville.

While working in Nashville, Jackson got the big break that was to secure his future, both in family and financial terms. He stayed at the boarding house of the widow of Major John Donelson and was soon attracted to her daughter Rachel, the estranged wife of Lewis Robards of Kentucky.

The Donelsons, Scots-Irish Presbyterians who moved from Gramoney between Larne and Carrickfergus in Co. Antrim in the early 18th century, were a family of substance in the region and Jackson's star rose considerably as he grew closer to Rachel and her family.

They were married in 1791, with Rachel unwittingly committing bigamy. Her husband had started divorce proceedings after they had parted, but had dropped these without Rachel knowing and it was two years into the marriage with Jackson before she learned of her dilemma.

Robards was now seeking a divorce, on the grounds of his wife's adultery and when it was granted Jackson and Rachel remarried. Divorce was uncommon in those days, but not entirely unheard of. And while Andrew and Rachel Jackson enjoyed a lot of love together, she had to endure much slander over her hurried second marriage.

The insults were even heaped on Jackson and, in 1806, it led him into a duel with a Charles Dickinson who had enraged Rachel about the marriage. Dickinson was to pay for the tirade with his life, something Jackson found difficult playing down in his later years of high office.

Like many other public figures of his time Jackson married above his station and this certainly made his path to the White House a little easier. He may have been the first prosecuting attorney for the region, but he had just barely qualified in law and the Donelson connection gave him the foothold to move up in the world.

Jackson's wealth increased when Rachel inherited a substantial amount of property and money from her father's estate. John Donelson had moved from Virginia to East Tennessee in 1779 and helped set up Sullivan county, and later Nashville. He was a navigator, explorer, merchant and magistrate. There may have been considerable wealth to go with the marriage, but it was a love match all right even though they had no children. After Rachel died, Jackson resisted the advances of many eligible women, and he never remarried.

During their marriage the pair adopted one of Rachel's nephews, an infant whom they called Andrew Jackson, Jun., and they also brought into their home a little Indian boy Lyncoya who had been abandoned in the battlefield in 1813 in the war with the Creek Indians. The boys brought a great fulfilment to Rachel's life and a comfort in the long periods when Andrew was away from home on political business. Sadly, Lyncoya died at the age of 16 from tuberculosis.

Rachel came from a family of 10 and the affluence Andrew married into was a quantum leap from the lifestyle of his parents back in Co. Antrim. The Donelsons were highly influential and Jackson was lucky and ambitious just when the state of Tennessee was being set up and he managed to align himself with one of the two strong political factions in the region.

Jackson sided with the faction of Tennessee Governor William Blount against the grouping of Revolutionary War hero John Sevier and for one so young, he picked up a lot of rewards: he served in the Constitutional Convention of Tennessee, was the first Congressman for the state in the US House of Representatives, and was elected a US senator, in 1823.

In 1804, the Jacksons were living at The Hermitage, outside Nashville, then a plantation log house and farm that was to make way for a luxury brick mansion and estate in 1819 which today bears glowing witness to the life and times of this illustrious Tennessean of first generation Scots-Irish Presbyterian extraction.

Seldom would Jackson have referred back to the roots of his parents and records show an almost total indifference to his family connections across the Atlantic. He did get letters from people in Ireland claiming kinship, but there is no evidence that he ever replied to them.

The only people from his family tree he ever kept in touch with were the Crawfords on his mother's side. They too were first generation Ulster Scots, but in those days in that part of the States the Scots-Irish were the local community and they had completely assimilated into American life.

In his earlier life, Jackson did not have much official church attachment - he would have been described as "a man of the Enlightenment" and what belief he had was of a Supreme Being out there somewhere. His deep interest in horse racing and breeding, coupled with a compulsiveness to dabble in the pursuit of gambling, left him a more worldly, than religious individual.

His dubious involvement in pistol duels left him open to much ridicule. Duelling was illegal in Tennessee and the participants had to go to Kentucky where one or other of them finished a dead man.

When Andrew Jackson returned from Washington after two terms as President, he changed and became very much what his late wife had been - a strongly evangelical Presbyterian. When he was President he refused to join the church, asserting that it would be looked upon as a political act if he did. When in Washington he enjoyed a long-standing friendship with the Roman Catholic bishop of Baltimore and paid pew rent to two churches there - First Presbyterian and St. John's Episcopal, and would show up frequently for services.

When he officially became a Presbyterian in 1838, Jackson said he would have joined the Church some time before but preferred to postpone the act until he had retired to the shades of private life.

As a soldier, Jackson had been major general of the militia in Tennessee since 1802 and he led his troops in battle in the war with the Creek Indians in 1812-13. His leadership qualities in battle earned him the nickname "Old Hickory" and after a number of significant successes over the Indians he returned to Nashville in triumph.

He was given the commission of major general in the US Army in May, 1814 and this took him to the Gulf Coast to face the British. He forced them back at Mobile, captured Pensacola and earned national acclaim by routing the Crown forces at the Battle of New Orleans on January 8, 1815, though the Treaty of Ghent, ending the war, had been signed on December 24, 1814.

This effectively finished British influence in the southern states and when hostilities ceased the US federal government called on Jackson to conduct the land negotiations with the Cherokee and Chickasaw Indian tribes. It was a task Jackson responded to enthusiastically and, by 1818, treaties with both tribes were concluded and it allowed the white settlers to move further west.

Jackson was also involved in moving the Seminole Indians out of Florida, ending Spanish rule there, and his last push as an Indian fighter came in 1820 when he completed a land treaty with the Choctaw tribe. This allowed Mississippi to be settled and become another state of the Union.

And Jackson it was who almost singlehandedly forged the American expansion in the early 19th century: removing the Indians from their lands; expelling the Spanish from the South and Southwest and ending British rule for ever in the country. He was a hero right across the States.

For a short period, he was Governor of Florida, but by 1821 he had returned to Nashville, relieved of his US Army commission, and ready to move for high political stakes. The journey to Washington was rough and, though he was backed by an influential Nashville grouping, he failed at the first attempt to defeat John Quincy Adams for the Presidency in 1824, winning the popular vote but losing out in the electoral college vote.

Jackson was again nominated as a Democrat in 1828 and in a dirty campaign his turbulent past and wife Rachel's bigamy figured prominently in attacks by the John Quincy Adams faction. This time, however, Jackson enjoyed a substantial victory on both the popular vote and the electoral college.

But the triumph was to be marred by tragedy. Six weeks after the election Rachel Jackson came across an opposition pamphlet highlighting the scandal of her double marriage and so distressed was she that she took to her bed and died on December 24, 1828. Jackson was devastated once again by a close family bereavement and he blamed his wife's death on the lies of his political enemies.

His journey to the White House had to be delayed and at 62 he took up Presidential office with a heavy heart. Rachel and he had been married for 35 years and Jackson found it difficult to come to terms with the fact that she had been taken from him just as he was about to assume the mantle of the nation's highest office.

Andrew served eight years as President - he won the 1832 election with a 55 per cent poll - and in that period spearheaded many major developments in the rapidly expanding states. The railroad was introduced and he became the first President to travel by train. He had his run-ins with the banks over monetary problems and there were bitter inter-party rivalries to sort out.

But it was the Indian re-settlements which caused the greatest upheaval during his Presidential term, given Jackson's deep-seated hostility to the tribes and his perusal of the rights of the white settlers.

He got Congress to pass legislation creating an Indian settlement west of the Mississippi River and to pass the Indian Removal Act. By 1834, Congress had established, through Jackson's prompting, the Indian Territory into which the five main tribes from the south east were moved. This pitiful trek by the tribes to a region that was later to become the state of Oklahoma is known in Indian folklore as "The Trail of Tears".

Just before he left office Jackson told the American people that he believed he had settled the Indian problem for all time and that he had saved the race from extinction. He said: "This unhappy race are now placed in a situation where we may well hope that they may share the blessings of civilisation and be saved from denigration and destruction to which they were rapidly hastening while they remained in the states.

"Our own citizens will rejoice that the remnant of that ill-fated race has been at last placed beyond the reach of injury or oppression and that the paternal care of the federal government will hereafter watch over them and protect them" . The Indian problem was far from being resolved, but Jackson returned to The Hermitage thinking that it was.

The two terms in the Presidency cost Jackson quite a lot in financial terms and when he returned from The White House to Tennessee in 1837 he was effectively broke. He remarked to friends that the several thousand dollars he had when he first went to Washington had been reduced to a few and to make ends meet he had to mortgage the annual cotton crop. The ailing finances left a much reduced inheritance for his adopted son Andrew Jackson Jun. and, when he sailed into a colossal 85,000 dollar debt 11 years after his father's death, The Hermitage had to be sold to the state.

In the last few years of Andrew Jackson's life he maintained a close interest in American national affairs and his imperialistic appetite was whetted by the successful annexation of Texas from the Mexicans and Oregon from the Indians. Jackson suffered greatly from bouts of tuberculosis during the years of his Presidency and worn out by a hyperactive life he died at The Hermitage on June 8, 1845, aged 78.

Today Jackson is looked back on as one of the finest of the American Presidents - a remarkable, highly versatile man who left an indelible mark in the various conquests that he tackled: law, soldiering and politics. He was a man of his times: an Indian fighter in the frontier who mercilessly pushed the tribes back; a Black slave owner who showed little sympathy for the plight of his slaves (he never emancipated one!); a purposely single-minded person who obviously made up his mind at an early age that he was never going to be poor and who developed a quick appreciation for good living and good clothes, and a politician who jealously guarded his constituency with the simple and sound philosophy "votes are votes". He was undoubtedly a man of the common people!

Jackson's love of the good life is illustrated by the fact that on his first trip to Philadelphia from the backwoods of Tennessee he purchased some relatively expensive clothes that allowed him to cut quite a dash back home. He also had an appreciation for the best wines. In Jackson's day there was quite a lot of social drinking and it was at these gatherings that much of the politicking was done.

Andrew and Rachel Jackson are buried in the grounds of The Hermitage, a place rich in historical treasures that is visited by 300,000 people every year. They may lie alongside one another, but Andrew's remains are curiously given more elevation than those of his wife. He is buried in a brick-lined vault with a concrete slab over the coffin. "Mrs. Jackson is buried in just dirt" - the slave Hannah from The Hermitage of the 1820s remarked when asked in the 1880s about how they were buried.

This bizarre comparison may tell its own story of one side of the Jackson characteristic, but it does not over-shadow the sterling qualities of a fearless first generation Ulsterman who more than any of his contemporaries helped make America great.

JAMES K. POLK

James Knox Polk - the 11th President of the United States - was very definitely Scots-Irish with ancestoral links to Paisley in Renfrewshire, Scotland and East Donegal in Ulster.

This well educated son of Presbyterian settlers followed in the Democratic tradition of Andrew Jackson and in his four-year term as President in 1845-49 he was responsible for extending the American borders to the north west through the settlement of the Oregon plains; the reannexation of Texas and the acquisition of California, with its rich gold finds.

It was a Presidency preoccupied with the Mexican war; the increasing friction between North and South which eventually led to the Civil War in 1862 and Polk's desire to build up a sound economic base for the American nation.

The Polks derive from an ancient Scottish family called Pollock or Pollok, who owned estates in Renfrewshire and Aberdeenshire. During the Scottish plantation of Ireland in the 17th century Sir Robert Bruce Pollock moved to the Lifford area of East Donegal and from this settlement he emigrated with his family across the Atlantic in 1680 to Somerset County in Maryland.

Robert and Magdalen Pollock (changed to Polk when they landed in America) had eight children and their offspring were to become some of the most distinguished men and women in the south west of America. James K. Polk was one such person. Records show that Robert Pollock had left valuable land in Ireland and it is significant that, in the will of his wife Magdalen (she died in 1724, predeceasing her husband by several years), she left her son Joseph "my estate Moerning Hall, in the kingdom of Ireland, and barony of Ross, County of Donegal, and in the parish of Leford".

Robert Polk was an elder in the old Rehobeth Presbyterian Church, claimed to be the oldest Presbyterian church in America. He brought with him from Ulster the family Bible, containing records of births and deaths; a clock purchased in Londonderry and an old mahogany case that contained 15 square bottles.

The Polk Bible was stained by the weather from being hidden in a tree, for the Ireland that the Polks left was a country in turmoil with the Protestant plantation settlers being put on to the defensive by the native Irish Roman Catholic population. This unrest was to culminate in the Siege of Londonderry in 1688-89, where the Protestants were besieged by the Jacobite forces led by King James II, and the Battle of the Boyne in 1690, which sealed the Glorious Settlement and the continuance of the Protestant Rule under William and Mary.

Many of the Polk connection moved to North Carolina, for they were a spirited people and saw great opportunity in the frontier lands of the Appalachians. Ezekiel Polk, a great grandson of Robert Polk, was a surveyor who was always seeking out land, and this adventurous zeal took him westwards to Tennessee, then a state in the making.

He first moved to Tennessee in 1790, but his wife's illness forced him to return to North Carolina. By 1803, he was back with several members of his family and a permanent Polk homestead was established on Carter's Creek, a few miles south of Franklin in middle Tennessee.

Ezekiel's son Samuel, also a surveyor of land, followed in 1806, with his very reluctant wife Jane Knox Polk, who thought a 500-mile journey into an unknown territory was a little bit much for her young family of four, who included the 11-year-old James Knox. It took six weeks for the journey by covered wagon from Mecklenburg County in North Carolina to middle-Tennessee, but on arrival Ezekiel presented Samuel with a generous portion of the land holdings. It was at a place called Duck River, close to the present-day town of Columbia in Maury County.

Maury County was a wilderness before 1800 - no white person would have come this way other than pioneering surveyors and hunters. The ordinary settlers could not have lived here, they would almost certainly have been killed by the Indians. The last Indian scalping took place in Maury County in 1804 and by 1806, when the Polks moved there, all of the Indian tribes would have been gone from the area.

The first settlers encountered a vast territory of virgin timber and canebrake - there were no open fields and everything had to be cleared. So when they bought a piece of land, the first thing they had to do was to procure an axe and clear enough log to build a home.

James K. Polk, in his diaries, mentions how when his family first arrived they initially had to clear the canebrake. The Polks may have been a family of substance, but in the frontier lands of Maury County they were no different from anyone else. They just had to take their coats off and work as hard as the rest, toiling in the land from dawn to dusk. Nothing came easy.

It took a war and money to move the Indians out of this part of Tennessee. The Shawnee aligned with the French and when the French lost the battle with the American forces the Indians were run out of the territory. Maury County was created, with Columbia the county seat, and waves of Scots-Irish settlers moved in such numbers that by 1830 the county was the third most populous in Tennessee.

Samuel Polk prospered with the development of Columbia, as a surveyor of lands and in business. Samuel's eldest son James Knox, named after his devout Presbyterian mother Jane Knox, was not considered as robust and as adventurous as his father and he was given a college education which prepared him for his entry into politics. He graduated with honours in mathematics and the classics and studied law in Nashville, where Andrew Jackson had become such a formidable man. After being admitted to the bar he opened a law office in Columbia and by 1820 he was elected to the Tennessee state legislature.

James K. Polk married Sarah Childress, the elder daughter of a wealthy Tennessee merchant, and her high intellect and stunning good looks complemented the Polk drive towards political stature. The wedding, in Spring Hill Presbyterian Church on January 1, 1824, was the highlight of the Nashville social calendar and, after a round of parties, they returned to Columbia to settle in a log cabin, near the Polk family home. A year later, Ezekiel Polk, the first of the clan to cross the Allegheny Mountains, died in West Tennessee, and left thousands of acres of frontier lands to his heirs.

Increasingly, James Polk came under the influence of Andrew Jackson and, after election to the United States House of Representatives, he stoutly defended "Old Hickory" when he was under investigation in Congress for allegedly killing six militia men during the Battle of New Orleans in 1815.

Polk served seven terms in Congress and in 1835 became Speaker of the House, the only President ever to hold that office. In 14 years he rarely missed a sitting and his assiduousness, and loyalty to Jackson, earned him the nickname "Young Hickory. He was Governor of Tennessee for one term, and was twice a defeated candidate. But his eye was on the Presidency and in 1845 he made it in a roundabout way.

Polk had been actively seeking the Democratic nomination for Vice-President, but when he called for the reannexation of Texas from the Mexicans and the Oregon territory as rightfully belonging to the American people he was widely seen as the man for the No.1 position.

The opposition came from James Buchanan, of Pennsylvania (of Co. Tyrone / Co. Donegal stock), Martin Van Buren, of New York; John C. Calhoun, of South Carolina (another Ulster-Scot) and Lewis Cass of Michigan. At the Democratic convention in Baltimore their challenge dissipated in a deadlock and Silas Wright of New York was nominated with Polk as his running mate. Wright declined to run and Polk was elected unanimously by the party delegates. The following November, he defeated Whig Henry Clay by only two electoral votes, the smallest margin of popular votes ever to elect a President up to that time.

James K. and Sarah Polk were hospitable hosts at the White House, laying on lavish receptions and social gatherings, for visiting dignatories, political friends and even opponents. The pair had no children, but both came from large families and they always had young people around them. Sarah was a very religious woman who had been a student of the Moravian Institute in North Carolina and though her husband had only a loose Presbyterian church connection he managed to attend church more often than any other President of his period.

Six days before his death in Nashville, on June 15, 1849, Polk was baptised by a Methodist minister. He died, aged 53, within four months of finishing his term as President and lies buried near the State Capital in Nashville. Sarah Polk lived for another 42 years with a niece whom she adopted as a daughter.

James K. Polk may have been an Andrew Jackson prodigy, but personally he was very different from Jackson. He was quiet, his mind was working all the time and he was very business-like in all his dealings. While the domineering Jackson wanted to push out into the frontier, Polk had a more reserved approach, although his success in widening the Union with the annexation of Texas, Oregon, California and New Mexico made him a President of relative greatness.

The Jacksonite Democratic decentralisation principles which Polk espoused championed the cause of the common man. Like Jackson,

Polk, when he returned from the White House, did not have much money. Presidential candidates personally financed their campaigns in those days and while Polk had a lot of land in West Tennessee he would not have been considered the richest of men.

Like his contemporaries, Polk was a slave owner and inherited several plantations in West Tennessee from his grandfather who had slaves. He was a man of his time, but when he reached the Presidency the slave issue was coming to a head and he had to take a more pragmatic approach on abolition.

James K. Polk set out his political stall in the footsteps of illustrious Tennessee politicians like Andrew Jackson, Davy Crockett and Sam Houston. Maury County was the political stomping ground of Crockett and Houston, with Columbia the place they would have done much of their politicking - in the town square. But whereas Crockett and Houston were pioneers and Indian fighters, as well as politicians, James K. Polk was solely political. He may have lived in Maury County when it was a rugged frontier, but his image is not of a man in buckskins with a long-barrelled rifle.

A letter written by Nathaniel Ewing in 1844 throws some light on the movement of some of the early Polks to America. Ewing wrote to a Polk connection : "Your forefathers and mine emigrated in the same ship from the North of Ireland in 1727, landed at New Castle and settled together in the upper part of Cecil County, adjoining the Pennsylvania Line and Lancaster County. There was a large colony composed principally of Ewings, Porters, Gillespies and Polks".

Another letter sent to President James Polk from a Mary Atherton in 1844 stated that her ancestor Robert Polk moved from Scotland to the North of Ireland after 1641 and his son James lived at Lisnefiffy, Co. Down, from where he removed to Charleston, South Carolina in 1738. This was not the President's family, but very probably relatives

ANDREW JOHNSON

Andrew Johnson - the man who rose to the United States Presidency with little or no education - came of Co. Antrim Presbyterian stock. His grandfather and namesake emigrated to America from the port of Larne about 1750 and Andrew was born at Raleigh in North Carolina in 1808.

The 17th President of the United States was reared on the wrong side of the tracks in a Carolina community which was known as "the poor Protestants". He managed to lift himself up by his bootlaces to become the third Tennessean to reach the White House. The rags to riches story began for Andrew Johnson at the age of three when his janitor father died: the little boy and his older brother were bound out to a tailor, to be fed and clothed for their work until they became 21.

The apprenticeship was not served to the full and when both boys ran away to South Carolina a reward of 10 dollars was put up for their capture. They returned to Raleigh for a time, but eventually both made it to East Tennessee and as a very young man Andrew opened a tailor's shop in Greeneville, a mountain town between Knoxville and Johnson City. There he married Eliza McCardle and she taught him to read and write. Johnson built up his business and began to take an interest in the politics of the region, following the Democratic line of another Tennessee President, James K. Polk. Eliza Johnson, who was also of Scots-Irish roots, was the driving force behind her husband's business and political career: she was considered a very astute, ambitious woman and Andrew would never have got to the White House without her push.

The couple eventually moved to Maury County in the centre of the lush farmlands of middle Tennessee. This was the homeland of James K. Polk and where men like Andrew Jackson, Davy Crockett and Sam Houston had considerable influence and, although a much younger man, Johnson learned his political acumen from the trail set in public life by the other four. Johnson, however, was not a typical southern Democrat, and when elected to the United States Senate he stood apart from the 21 other senators from the South in opposing the secession from the Union on the abolition of slavery issue.

Abraham Lincoln saw in Andrew Johnson a man who could help bring the South along in his move to abolish slavery, but while Johnson succeeded Lincoln to the Presidency in 1865 at the end of the Civil War he became a figure of much ridicule on both sides of the Mason /Dixon line (the North-South divide).

For his Union tendencies, Johnson was called "a homemade Yankee" by Southerners; "white trash" and "a traitor". To many Northerners he was "a turncoat". In Tennessee, Johnson had many enemies and the only place he enjoyed real popular support was in the eastern region. At President Lincoln's request Johnson left the Senate to become military governor of Tennessee and while serving in that post he was nominated Vice-President.

It was on his inauguration as Vice-President that Andrew Johnson was unfairly branded by his enemies as a drunkard. Shortly before the ceremonies he took ill and asked for a stimulant. He drank three glasses of brandy and when he reached the Senate Chamber the alcohol and the intense heat of a crowded room made him give a rambling, incoherent speech. In truth, Johnson was a moderate drinker, but he never lived down the after-effects of those three glasses of brandy.

Johnson's mind was a sponge and he regularly took part in student debates, even though he himself was not a student. He was a self taught man. When he became President, Johnson increased his unpopularity in the South by insisting on personally punishing the Confederate leaders and economically penalising the southern states. Colleagues managed to get him to soften this line and a Proclamation of Amnesty was issued which gave a general pardon to all in the Confederate rebellion, provided they took an oath of allegiance to the Union. A total of 14,000 southerners received pardons.

The Civil War had created immense political and economic problems, none the least making the Southern states bankrupt and having four million black slaves freed, all of them badly needing education, housing and employment.

Johnson became increasingly more conciliatory towards the South and he tried to rally the east and mid-west of the country against demands for severe punishment of the southern states. Joining him in this crusade was General Ulysses S. Grant, the triumphant commander of the Union Army, and ominously it was Johnson who got the jeers, Grant the cheers. Later Johnson suffered more humiliation when impeachment charges were levelled against him for "high crimes and misdemeanours". This involved difficulties Johnson experienced with his Secretary of War, Edwin M. Stanton, a radical Republican.

The full Senate met for the trial on May 26, 1868 and voted 35 in favour of conviction and 19 against. It was just one vote short of the necessary two-thirds - by the slimmest of margins Johnson was acquitted. Soon after, his Presidential term ended, but he was to return to Washington in 1875 when the people of Tennessee elected him to the Senate. He was the only former President to serve as Senator. In the same year, this most unpopular President died suddenly at the home of his daughter at Carter Station, Tennessee. He had had a stroke which mainly affected his left side, rendering him unconscious. He was 67.

Johnson had been a man of solid build, about five feet nine inches - with an Indian-like swarthiness, black hair, deep-set dark eyes and an expression of grim determination which personified his Scots-Irish characteristic. His wife Eliza's health had deteriorated by the time he had reached the White House and she was so weakened by tuberculosis that she made only one public appearance during her four years' residence there. A married daughter Martha Johnson Patterson carried out the First Lady duties.

The successor to Andrew Johnson in the Presidency was his main military confidante Ulysses Simpson Grant, whose mother Hannah Simpson was descended from the Simpson family of Dergenagh near Dungannon, Co. Tyrone. Her great-grandfather John Simpson had left Ulster in 1760. Grant was the 18th President, a republican who served from 1869 to 1877.

Andrew Johnson, the tailor turned politician, may have had a tumultuous Presidential term, but, elected after the assassination of Abraham Lincoln and at the end of a bloody Civil War, he inherited the almost impossible task of trying to unite a nation irrevocably split into two warring factions.

As a Southerner despised by many of his own people and mistrusted by elements in the North, Johnson found the going tough. But his four difficult years in the White House could never disguise the fact that a man from such humble beginnings could aspire to the highest office in the land, and without any formal education. The humble wooden shack where Andrew Johnson was born still stands today at Raleigh in North Carolina. His memory lives on!

•••

• **President Bill Clinton:** the present occupant at the White House, claims his ancestors on his mother's side were Scots-Irish, coming from Co. Fermanagh and bearing the name of Cassidy. This link has yet to be positively verified.

9

Knoxville: *a city founded by Ulstermen*

KNOXVILLE - third largest city in Tennessee with a population of 165,000 - was founded by James White, an Ulster-Scots Presbyterian frontiersman whose father was born in Londonderry. Two hundred years ago the thriving capital of the Tennessee Valley region sprouted from the turnip patches of this hardy settler who set up home on the banks of the Holston River, now the Tennessee River.

White was the first of many Scots-Irish to settle in the region and his activities as a soldier, civic leader and church member were inspirational to others of his Presbyterian kinsfolk in illustriously carving a niche in this part of the frontier state. Their achievements are recorded for posterity, not just for the benefit of the mass of Knoxville people with Scots-Irish roots, but for their distant cousins across in Northern Ireland and Scotland.

JAMES WHITE (1747-1821)

Revolutionary war hero and the founder of Knoxville General James White had very strong Scots-Irish blood in his veins. His people - of the Campbell clan - had originally lived at Inveraray and Lochgoilhead in Argyllshire on the western lowlands of Scotland and it was his grandfather Moses White who moved to Co. Londonderry with his wife Mary Campbell in the latter part of the 17th century.

They had seven children, one of them Moses White II (James White's father), who was to leave Ireland in 1741 and settle in Lancaster County, Pennsylvania. Moses White II married Mary McConnell and they moved to Iredell (Rowan County) in North Carolina. James was the fourth of their six children. He married Mary Lawson from North Carolina, and they had three sons and four daughters.

In the Revolutionary War James White captained the North Carolina militia and it was this service which entitled him to a grant of land which he eventually was to select along the banks of the Holston River, now the Tennessee River which flows through Knoxville. However, before the final settlement he spent several years in Virginia and was a member of the general assembly of the state of Franklin which met in Jonesboro and was speaker of the senate.

When White and his family first moved to the Holston River basin in 1785 his home was a modest log cabin with an adjoining turnip patch, but a year later he had a two-storey blockhouse built, to be known as White's Fort. Settlers' homes needed to be well fortified in those days due to the threats from marauding Cherokee Indians and White's Fort came under attack on numerous occasions.

White became a highly influential man in this part of the frontier: in 1789 he was a representative from Hawkins County in the legislature of North Carolina and was a member of the convention which ratified the constitution of the United States.

In 1790, during the organisation of the territory of the United States south of the River Ohio by Governor William Blount, White was appointed major of the militia and justice of the peace of Hawkins County. He was involved with Blount in talks with the Cherokee Indians which led to the signing of the Holston Treaty on July 2, 1791. This authorised the purchase of all the lands of present-day Knoxville and the surrounding Knox/County from the Indians - an area of some 1,260 square miles.

In October, 1791, to White, was given the task of laying out Knoxville as a proper settlement and it was agreed to name it in honour of General Henry Knox, the Secretary of War, a man of Co. Down pedigree. Knoxville was then in a thicket of brushwood and grapevines, except a small portion in front of the river where all the business was done.

The original 64 lots of land, arranged by White's son-in-law and surveyor Charles McClung, were chosen by lottery at a price of eight dollars for each half-acre. Demand by the incoming settlers was brisk - the great city of Knoxville was indeed taking shape with an original 10 streets.

White was promoted to lieutenant colonel commandant in the militia and it was his obvious gifts of sympathy, understanding, patience and tact which earned him the chairmanship of the court of pleas and quarter sessions, the body appointed to fairly monitor the allocation of land lots.

The conflict between the impetuous settlers and the Indian community continued, but White succeeded in keeping a cool head and built up a trust with the Indian tribesmen. His half-sister Sarah, wife of Joseph Wilson, and her children were captured by Creek Indians in Sumner County in middle Tennessee, but after great effort, White succeeded in ransoming all of them. An Indian chief said that "the Great Spirit" aided in the rescue of the last little Wilson girl because of James White's goodness.

In another incident, Governor Blount despatched James White to disperse a large force of settlers ready to march upon Indian settlements and it took much dialogue before the tension was defused. White did help to thwart attacks on Knoxville by the Cherokee and Creek tribes - he stood by the defence of his people at all times.

White later became a brigadier general in the militia and he helped negotiate the treaty with the Cherokees wherby the Indians received 5,000 dollars and an annuity of 1,000 dollars for their lands. In the Creek War he led 850 men from Tennessee to Alabama to help Andrew Jackson in the fight against the Indians.

James White was a staunch Presbyterian and was a founding elder of Lebanon in the Fork Presbyterian Church, the first church organised in the Knoxville region. He was also a founding elder of First Knoxville Presbyterian Church, giving over his turnip patch for the Church building and the adjoining cemetery. He also gave the land for Blount College, later to become the University of Tennessee.

He was a member of the Territorial House of Representatives and when Tennessee was being prepared for admission into the Union as a state he was the Knox County member of the constitutional convention. He served several terms as state senator and senate speaker.

White and his wife Mary are buried in the First Presbyterian cemetery and a tribute pens the appropriate words: "Of James White as a soldier, citizen, official and Christian nothing needs to be added to the bare record of his services to his home, country and church".

The Knoxville Register of August 21, 1821, in its obituary of General James White, said that in civil, military and ecclesiastical concerns he had taken a distinguished part. "He has acquitted himself with fidelity and usefulness, in the numerous public functions in which he has been called upon to act. This town, particularly, has cause to remember him with gratitude and veneration. He was its founder and patron and ever watched over its interests with the affection of a parent".

CHARLES McCLUNG (1761-1835)

Surveyor, merchant and lawyer Charles McClung was born in Lancaster, Pennsylvania, the son of Matthew McClung, a native of the North of Ireland, and wife Martha Cunningham. Charles spent most of his early life working on his father's farm and was engaged in business in Philadelphia for a time. But like his contemporaries he found the appeal of the frontier compelling and after moving through the Shenandoah valley in Virginia he came upon White's Fort, on the present site of the city of Knoxville.

City founder James White was a Presbyterian kinsman and McClung married his eldest daughter Margaret and with his father-in-law really set about developing the Holston River basin which encompassed Knoxville. The fact that the streets of Knoxville were named after those in Philadelphia was due to McClung's influence as the city's first surveyor and from 1792 to 1834 he held the clerkship of the first Knox County court. He was a member of the convention which met in Knoxville in 1796 to form the constitution for the new state of Tennessee and along with Revolutionary War hero William Blount drafted the constitution.

McClung, a major in the cavalry regiment for the territory, was also one of Knoxville's leading businessmen, right up until his death. He was described as a man of fine personal appearance and of an able and discriminating mind. Many of Knoxville's most distinguished citizens were descended from Charles McClung.

Calvin Morgan McClung (1855-1919) was a leading businessman and collector of local historical materials. The grandson of Charles McClung, Judge Hugh Lawson McClung (1858-1936) served as a justice in the Tennessee supreme court and chancellor of the chancery division of Knox County. He was a trustee of the University of Tennessee for 23 years, as his father and grandfather had been.

JOHN ADAIR (1732-1827)

Ballymena, Co. Antrim-born John Adair played a key role in defeating the British at the Battle of Kings Mountain in October, 1780 but he did not join the Overmountain Men in their epic struggle.

John was, more than anyone else, responsible for raising the finance to arm and supply the militia which confronted Colonel Patrick Ferguson and his army of Redcoats. By a strange twist of fate, he was the man of the hour. As land entry taker for the state of North Carolina John was in possession of 12,735 dollars - a lot of money in those days - when his fellow Wataugans (mainly Scots-Irish settlers) were being over-run by the British forces.

The Revolutionary forces were very short of money and though John knew that the cash he possessed belonged to the state, he succumbed to the persuasion of the Watauga leaders John Sevier and Isaac Shelby to hand it over for patriotic uses.

John, in normal times a law-abiding citizen, reasoned with his action thus: "Colonel Sevier, I have no authority by law to make this disposition of the money. It belongs to the impoverished treasury of North Carolina and I dare not appropriate a cent of it to any purpose. But if the country is over-run by the British, our liberty is gone. Take it, if the enemy, by its use, is driven from the country, I can trust that country to justify and vindicate my conduct. So take it".

Sevier and Shelby took the money, with the promise to re-pay it out of their own pockets if the North Carolina legislature considered Adair's act illegal. When the legislature met in 1782, the action of all three men was upheld. The money purchased much-needed guns and ammunition and after Kings Mountain the war was effectively over for the British.

Adair, living in Sullivan County in North Carolina (today a part of Tennessee), served as a volunteer in the militia and saw action against both the British and their then allies the Indians. He later became a scout, prowling the Virginian wilderness, spying on the Indian tribes for payment of a mere 1.50 dollars a day - money he was never to receive for his hazardous work.

Very little is known of John Adair's life in the north of Ireland, but it has been established he grew up at Ballee, a townland in present-day Ballymena, Co. Antrim. Two personal account books have been located bearing his signature which show that he lived for a time in Belfast. The date of one of the books is 1766; the other 1776 and it clearly points to the fact that he was in America at the time.

John was 18 when he left the north of Ireland with his family. They landed at Baltimore and lived for about a year in Maryland, another year in Pennsylvania, before making the long trek to Sullivan County. After the Revolutionary War he received a 640-acre land grant in Knox County and with his wife Ellen Crawford Adair, he built Adair Station, a forted home about five miles north of White's Fort, now downtown Knoxville. He was the commissioner responsible with the furnishing of provisions for the Cumberland Guards, a company of armed escorts who saw settlers safely across the then wilderness from Knoxville to Nashville. Adair Station doubled up as a home and a storehouse for these provisions.

Adair became a justice of the peace for Knox County and a trustee of Blount College. He represented his county at the 1796 State Constitutional Convention in Knoxville and with fellow Ulster-Scots James White and George McNutt was present at the birth of Tennessee. He too was a founding elder in First Knoxville Presbyterian Church and a plaque today stands in the church grounds to himself, James White and George McNutt.

John Adair was 95 when he died on February 24, 1827. The death notice in the Knoxville Register was recorded thus: "Died, on February 24, 1827 at his residence in this County, John Adair Esq., at the advanced age of 95. He was among the early settlers in this County, a man of enterprise and respectability, for many years an elder in the Presbyterian Church; unblemished in his deportment with the world, and continued to the end to evince the integrity of his heart and sincerity of his profession".

GEORGE McNUTT (1751-1823)

This native of Co. Antrim was a patriot in the Revolutionary War against the British, a hero of the Battle of Kings Mountain on October

7, 1780. George first settled in Virginia on arrival from Ireland and moved to a settlement close to the French Broad River in East Tennessee, known as the "Irish Bottom" for its preponderance of Scots-Irish families.

When he moved to the Holston River region just above Knoxville he became a contemporary of James White, the founder of Knoxville, and together they served as elders in the first church in the region - Lebanon in the Fork Presbyterian.

George, with his clear melodious voice, was the church's main precentor and he also was an elder in First Knoxville Presbyterian Church. He was a justice of the peace in Knoxville and one of the first commissioners of Knox County. His interest in education brought appointments as charter trustee of several leading academies, including Blount College.

MAJOR-GENERAL HENRY KNOX (1750-1806)

Henry Knox, the seventh son of William Knox who emigrated to Boston from Co. Down in 1729, is acknowledged as being one of the leading patriots and military strategists in American history.

In military service from an early age, Henry Knox became a close friend and associate of General George Washington and after distinguishing himself in a number of battles was commissioned as a brigadier-general. He contributed to the capture of General Cornwallis at Yorktown in 1781 during the Revolutionary War by placing the American cannon in the most effective position. That year he became major-general and was involved in the establishment of the first American military academy, with George Washington as president and himself as secretary.

Knox within a short time was Secretary of War and his service in administering the problems of the frontier settlements was recognised when James White, encouraged by Governor William Blount, named Knoxville in his honour. The surrounding county was also given the name Knox. The successful negotiation of land treaties with the Indians was a landmark in Knox's career and his leadership contributed to the rapid expansion of the frontiers. Knox never visited Tennessee.

ROBERT J. McKINNEY (1803-1875)

Distinguished lawyer and judge Robert McKinney was born in Coleraine, a member of a prominent Ulster family who moved to America at the beginning of the 19th century.

Robert was a very small boy when his father Dr. Samuel McKinney left Ireland with his family in 1809 and after passing through Philadelphia they settled on a farm at Rogersville in East Tennessee. There, young Robert was able to combine his studies for the law with the tasks of the family farm. An uncle John Augustine McKinney was the leading lawyer in Rogersville at the time and this allowed him to easily move into the legal sphere.

He was licensed in 1824 and soon became circuit lawyer for three counties in East Tennessee. His legal skills were acclaimed throughout Tennessee and in 1847 he was elevated as a judge of the Supreme Court of the State. McKinney held this position until 1861 when the courts were closed because of the Civil War and he was subsequently despatched to Washington as a peace commissioner. Judge McKinney opposed the War, but when Tennessee seceded from the Union he remained loyal to his State.

Described as a man of sound judgment and good business ability; he was thorough and accurate as a lawyer; sedate and dignified in manner; strict in business matters, but kind and generous. He was married twice: to the daughters of the Rev. Charles Coffin - Margaret, who died two years after the wedding in 1843, and Mary, whom he wed in 1851. He was a loyal member of First Knoxville Presbyterian Church and is buried in the city's Greenwood Cemetery.

THOMAS WILLIAM HUMES (1815-1892)

Thomas William Humes was born in Knoxville into a strong Presbyterian family, but became one of the leading Episcopal (Anglican) clerics in East Tennessee in the 19th century. His father Thomas was an Armagh man who had moved to America when a boy - his mother Margaret Russell was born in Jefferson County in Tennessee, like her husband a devout Presbyterian, of Scots-Irish roots.

Thomas W. graduated from East Tennessee College in 1831; received a master's degree in 1833 and, complying with his mother's wishes that he should become a Presbyterian minister, studied theology at Princeton. His move towards the ministry was cut short however, when he found he could not subscribe to the Westminster Confession of Faith. He returned to develop a business career in Knoxville.

Humes eventually turned to journalism and he edited in succession The Knoxville Times, the Knoxville Register and The Watch Tower, a Whig campaign paper. Never far removed from church life, Humes was ordained as a deacon in the Episcopal Church in 1845 and within a year was appointed rector of St. John's parish in downtown Knoxville. He held this position until 1861, when he resigned over his sympathy for the Union cause in the Civil War. He was reinstated in 1863 when the Union Army occupied Knoxville and served another six years.

Humes became president of East Tennessee University and over an 18-year period he restored the institution to a high standing after the chaos of the Civil War. The grounds and buildings of the University were occupied in succession by the Confederate and Union armies during the War.

He was the author of the book "The Loyal Mountaineers"; president of the Knoxville Bible Society; a member of the Sons of Temperance; a missionary of the Episcopal Church in East Tennessee in 1884-86 and librarian at the Lawson McGhee Library in Knoxville during the last six year of his life. Thomas William Humes was one of Knoxville's most accomplished clerics, educationalists and journalists.

JAMES PARK (1822-1912)

Presbyterian minister the Rev. James Park was also one of Knoxville's foremost clerics in the 19th century, like Thomas William Humes the son of a native-born Ulsterman.

James Park Snr. moved to America from the north of Ireland in 1796 and with his brother William settled in Knoxville, where they were prosperously engaged in the mercantile business. He was an elder in First Knoxville Presbyterian Church, a trustee of East Tennessee College and twice Mayor of Knoxville (1818-1821 and 1824-26).

James, the 11th of 12 children, was a graduate of East Tennessee University and Princeton College and in 1848 was ordained for the ministry. In between holding pastorates at First Rogersville and First Knoxville Churches, James Park was for a time co-principal of the

Knoxville Female Seminary and principal of the Tennessee School for the Deaf.

He was appointed a trustee of East Tennessee University, which became the University of Tennessee, and in 1890 was elected Moderator of the General Assembly of the Presbyterian Church, often referred to as the Southern Presbyterian Church in the United States. He maintained the link with First Knoxville congregation until his death and was the author of the Church's history in 1876.

ARCHIBALD ROANE (1759-1819)

A Judge and the second Tennessee state governor, Archibald Roane was the son of Andrew Roane, a weaver to trade who came to America from Ulster in 1739 with his wife Margaret (nee Walker).

Archibald's parents both died when he was a boy and he was cared for by his Presbyterian minister uncle the Rev. John Roane at the family settlement in Lancaster, Pennsylvania. He fought in the Revolutionary War with the Lancaster County militia against the British and was present at the surrender of General Cornwallis in 1781. By 1784 Roane was a professor of languages and mathematics at Liberty Hall Academy in Lexington, Virginia and when he moved to Tennessee in 1788 he practised law in Washington County, then in North Carolina.

Roane represented Jefferson County in the Knoxville convention which framed the constitution of the new state of Tennessee in 1796 and served as a superior court judge for six years. His election as state governor in 1801 was overseen by Andrew Jackson and he served two years before being defeated by John Sevier, the Revolutionary War hero. He took no further part in politics, but remained a circuit judge until shortly before his death.

CHARLES McCLUNG McGHEE (1828-1907)

This eminent Tennessee financier was the great grandson of a native-born Ulster couple who settled in Lancaster County, Pennsylvania about 1746. His grandfather Barclay McGhee moved to East Tennessee in 1787 and when his father John died, Charles M. inherited about 15,000 acres of land in the Little Tennessee River valley.

He married Isabella White, a great grand-daughter of James White, the founder of Knoxville, but she passed on within a year leaving a son who died in infancy. McGhee married Cornelia White, a sister, and they had five children.

During the Civil War, he served as a staff officer and was a colonel in the commissary department of the Confederate Army, based in Knoxville. When the War ended McGhee ran the People's Bank of Knoxville and developed extensive coal and railroad interests in East Tennessee. He was responsible for the building of the Knoxville-Ohio rail network and set up links with the railways in Georgia and Virginia. For many years Charles McGhee was trustee, treasurer and secretary of the University of Tennessee. The Lawson McGhee Library in Knoxville is named after his daughter.

HUGH LAWSON WHITE (1773-1840)

The son of James White, the founder of Knoxville, was one of Tennessee's best-known lawyers in the early part of the 19th century. He reached Supreme Court Judge status in 1814, served as a United States senator and was a Presidential candidate in 1836, losing in a bitter fight to Andrew Jackson's hand-picked man Martin Van Buren.

White was married to Elizabeth Moore Carrick, daughter of the Rev. Samuel Carrick, minister of Lebanon in the Fork and First Knoxville Presbyterian Churches.

GEORGE McNUTT WHITE (1800-1878)

This grandson of the early Scots-Irish pioneers James White and George McNutt was Mayor of Knoxville in 1852-53. He was also sheriff of Knox County; county court clerk and circuit court clerk. In keeping with family tradition he was an elder in First Knoxville Presbyterian Church and married a sister of Dr. James Park, the minister there for 50 years.

REV. SAMUEL GRAHAM RAMSEY (1771-1817)

One of the earliest of preachers in Tennessee, Samuel Ramsey was of second generation Scots-Irish descent. He ministered with several congregations in East Tennessee, including for a time First Knoxville. He also ran a preparatory school for boys.

ROBERT HOUSTON (1765-1834)

This Secretary of State for Tennessee, state senator and the first sheriff of Knox County was born in South Carolina, of Scots-Irish parents. He came to Tennessee about 1790 and within two years he was commissioned by Governor William Blount as sheriff of Knox County. As the chief lawman, he opened the first county court and jailhouse and he helped defend Knoxville from repeated Indian attack.

Houston's remit in the county increased when he became tax assessor, and he later served the US federal Government as paymaster of the troops stationed in East Tennessee. He also played a key role in the various land treaties negotiated with the Cherokee Indians.

JAMES DARDIS (1766-1846)

Southern Ireland-born James Dardis, one of the few Roman Catholics living in Knoxville at the beginning of the 19th century, was highly regarded by his Scots-Irish Presbyterian neighbours as "a substantial and influential citizen".

Born in Bellinac, West-Meath, James Dardis emigrated to America with his brothers Edward and Thomas and had settled on 200 acres in Hawkins county, East Tennessee in 1796. He was a lieutenant in the Cavalry Volunteers and moved to Knoxville with his family in 1800. His brother Thomas became a prominent Knoxville lawyer and was killed in a pistol duel with a General John Cocke of Grainger county.

James Dardis was licensed as a merchant on Cumberland Street, owning 722 acres by 1812, and his estate expanded considerably when his brother died. He served on the board of the Bank of Tennessee in Knoxville, along with Hugh Lawson White, James Park and others, and became a member of the Tennessee legislature.

Dardis was a close associate of James White, the founder of Knoxville, and in the celebration of the Fourth of July anniversary in 1808, White was the committee president and Dardis vice-president, with Revolutionary War hero John Sevier honorary president for the day.

With few Roman Catholics living in Knoxville in the early part of the 19th century, it was difficult to establish a proper church and priests had to be brought in from Kentucky on an occasional basis to conduct mass. In his later life, James Dardis moved to Winchester, Franklin county in middle Tennessee and it was not until construction work on the railroads began in the 1840s that Roman Catholics came into Knoxville in sufficient numbers to establish a proper church and hold regular services.

Though Dardis was a devout Roman Catholic, his daughters were married in First Knoxville Presbyterian Church and they and their off-spring became members of that denomination. James Dardis died at Winchester on Christmas Day, 1846 and in his obituary it was said he was trusted with positions of high responsibility because of "his honesty and good judgment".

THE DUNLAPS

One of the first citizens of Knoxville was Hugh Dunlap, born in Londonderry in 1760 and a settler who moved from Philadelphia to the Holston/French Broad Rivers in 1791-92 when James White was founding his township.

Hugh opened a dry goods store in Knoxville and married Suzanna Gilliam, daughter of Deveraux Gilliam, a French Huguenot who had settled east of Knoxville in 1785. The couple's first son was Robert Gilliam Dunlap, who became acquainted with Andrew Jackson and served in his escort company during the Seminole War.

R.G. reached the rank of general in the Tennessee militia before moving to Texas, then a republic. Under President Mirabeau Lamar he was treasurer of the Texas Republic in 1839 and was Minister to the United States in 1840. A younger brother, Hugh White Dunlap was a lawyer and planter and served for a time in the Tennessee state legislature, and as grand master of the Masonic Order in Nashville.

He was a lieutenant colonel in the Mexican War with the 5th Louisiana Volunteer Infantry and died of yellow fever at the Battle of New Orleans in 1815. He had estates in Louisiana and Mississippi. Hugh's twin brother Richard was a member of the United States Congress with Davy Crockett, both men representing West Tennessee districts.

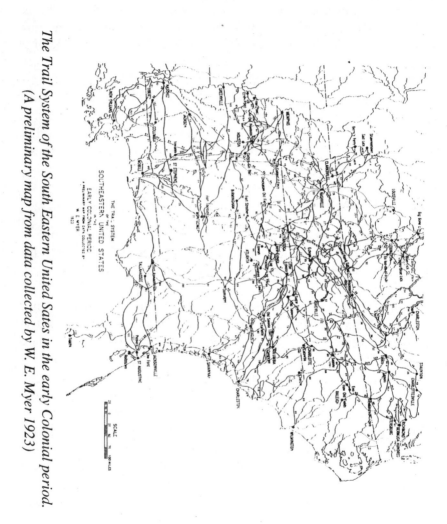

The Trail System of the South Eastern United Sates in the early Colonial period.
(A preliminary map from data collected by W. E. Myer 1923)

10

Heroics *in the founding of Nashville*

Three men with strong Scots-Irish connections were the founding
fathers of Nashville, today the capital of Tennessee and a teem-
ing modern metropolis with a population of half a million.

James Robertson, John Donelson and Richard Henderson planned
and set up the Cumberland settlement in the severe winter of 1779-80
as the westernmost frontier post on the American continent. It was an
exploit noted for its heroism and courage.

The pioneering settlement, on the banks of the Cumberland River in
middle Tennessee, was named Fort Nashborough, after Revolutionary
War hero General Francis Nash, of North Carolina, and the first settlers
numbered several hundred hardy souls who had come from the Carolinas,
Virginia and Pennsylvania. Scots-Irish families formed a large part of
the early Nashborough settlement, with most of the men fresh from
soldiering in the Revolutionary War, anxious to take advantage of the
land grants on offer to them. James Robertson (1742-1814) was a second generation Ulsterman whose immigrant family had moved to North
Carolina in the mid-18th century via the valley of Virginia. Robertson
helped form, in the early 1770s, the Watauga Association - the first
white settlement in what is today north east Tennessee - and, within a
year of putting down his roots at Fort Nashborough, he and his brother
Charles were doing their bit for the Revolutionary cause at the Battle of
Kings Mountain.

John Donelson was a member of a Presbyterian family from
Gramoney, a townland south of Larne and close to Carrickfergus in

Co. Antrim. Some of the Donelson clan (today in Northern Ireland they would be known as Donaldson) moved to America via the port of Larne about 1740 and they too reached North Carolina via the valley of Virginia.

Donelson, a Colonel in the Revolutionary Army, was also a boat builder and navigator of some skill and it was he who piloted the settlers on their hazardous river trip in December, 1779, from Fort Patrick Henry in East Tennessee to Fort Nashborough. On board one of the boats on that fateful trip was Colonel Donelson's 13-year-old daughter Rachel, who was later to become the wife of General Andrew Jackson, the seventh President of the United States.

Richard Henderson was a North Carolina lawyer and land agent who worked closely with Daniel Boone, the English pioneer, in settling families along the frontier. Like Robertson and Donelson his roots were Scots-Irish.

John Donelson is intrinsically linked to probably the most daring feat of navigation ever tackled in the settling of America's frontier region, but the irony was that, when his mission was successfully accomplished, Donelson was killed several years later during an Indian raid in Kentucky. His friend, James Robertson managed to live long enough to see Nashville (Fort Nashborough) grow to become one of Tennessee's leading centres of population.

Moves to settle the Cumberland River region of middle Tennessee began in 1777 in a plan drawn up in East Tennessee by James Robertson, John Donelson and Richard Henderson. Robertson led an exploratory team of nine to the region in the winter of 1778-79 and after looking over the land there was general agreement that it was ripe for settlement. A 3,000-acre grant was negotiated and arrangements made for the movement of those families who were prepared to take a chance and start a new life in the rugged wilderness beyond.

The journey was divided into two: Robertson and his men would take the animals (horses, cows, pigs and sheep) and other belongings; Donelson would ferry the women and children on a flotilla of flat wooden boats. Robertson and 200 men and boys travelled the Kentucky route, along Wilderness Road and through the Cumberland Gap, starting out from Big Creek on the Holston River in East Tennessee in the autumn of 1779. The extreme cold winter made the 400-mile journey difficult, with deep snow and frozen rivers contributing to a tortuous trek for almost three months.

By Christmas week of 1779 they arrived at their destination, worn out but excited with the prospect that a new settlement was in sight. The Cumberland River was frozen over and to reach the point Robertson had marked out on his original surveying mission, the animal stock had to be driven across the rock solid ice.

The Cumberland settlement took root on Christmas Day, 1779 and right away James Robertson and his men set about erecting log cabins and clearing stretches of land for the arrival of John Donelson and the families by boat.

A party of 300 people, mostly women and children, left Fort Patrick Henry and moved down the Holston River in an armada of little flat boats. It was a journey into the unknown; along unchartered waters, over dangerous shoals, rapids and falls, through territory where hostile Indians lived and in weather conditions in which only the toughest survived.

After a journey of only three miles Donelson's voyage came to an abrupt halt; ice and cold had set in and the frozen river made progress impossible. There was no movement until mid-February and when the boats did eventually cut loose they were hampered again by the swell of the river, due to the incessant heavy rain.

A few boats sank and some of the voyagers contracted the smallpox epidemic and died. As they passed through the Chickamauga Indian territory the boats came under attack from tribesmen massed on the shore. There were casualties on both sides, with the settlers countering the Indian assaults with sniper fire from their Kentucky long rifles.

A few boats dragged behind, some sank or fell into Indian hands, but most kept doggedly along, with the voyagers determined to reach the Cumberland settlement by the Springtime. Gradually they got past the danger points and on March 15 reached the mouth of the Tennessee River and the high water of the Ohio River. The flat boats were totally unsuited for the upstream currents and this further hampered progress.

Supplies were running short and it was necessary to make camp for a period until food supplies could be obtained by hunting buffalo and bear in the surrounding forests. Replenished, the families embarked on the last stage of their journey - slowly up the Cumberland River to the promised land surveyed by James Robertson.

They eventually arrived at French Salt Lick (the site of present-day down-town Nashville) on Monday April 24, 1780 and were warmly greeted by James Robertson and his men, who had been toiling away feverishly since Christmas to make the region habitable for the expected influx of their kinfolks.

The perilous river journey from Fort Patrick Henry to Fort Nashborough covered 985 miles. It was a human ordeal of great magnitude and though a few dozen of the brave pioneers did not reach the final destination - they either died of smallpox or were killed by Indians - those who did found their sacrifice had been well worthwhile.

Within days, eight station settlements had sprouted up on the banks of the Cumberland River, with Fort Nashborough the largest. James Robertson had prepared the ground well and with the help of John Donelson and Colonel Richard Henderson, known to his contemporaries as "Carolina Dick", he established the Cumberland Association, along the same lines as the Watauga Association set up in East Tennessee eight years earlier. As in Watauga, the Scots-Irish were a predominant strain in the Cumberland settlement.

The eight Cumberland stations were: Fort Nashborough, Mansker's Lick, Bledsoe's, Asher's, Stone's River, Freeland's, Eaton's and Fort Union. Nashville had come into being and within 20 years this smattering of simple log cabins, one-acre plots and fortified look-outs (required to resist Indian attacks) had expanded to become a leading township in Tennessee.

Robertson, Donelson and Henderson were the founding fathers of Nashville but in 1788 there arrived in the region a young man of Ulster-born parents who was to guide the destiny of Nashville, Tennessee and the United States until well into the 19th century.

The quality of life in Nashville and the Cumberland River settlement attracted Andrew Jackson and through his influence over the next 40 years the region carved for itself a considerable niche on the map of the United States. By 1810, Nashville had grown to a sizeable town. More turmoil was to follow in the 1860s years of the American Civil War, but Nashville was evolving as a most important strategic centre of the State. James Robertson, John Donelson and Richard Henderson had indeed planted real seed when they founded Fort Nashborough.

11

Scots-Irish *who framed the Declaration of Independence*

At least eight of the 56 signatories of the American Declaration of Independence were of the Scots-Irish tradition. The Declaration, signed in Philadelphia on July 4, 1776, was a statement which enshrined much of the independent and democratic spirit that had been brought to America by the Presbyterian settlers from Ulster.

Thomas Jefferson from Virginia drafted the Declaration and the task of transcribing the document went to Charles Thompson, a native of Maghera in Co. Londonderry. Thompson held the high rank of Perpetual Secretary to the Continental Congress in America, the legislature which was then the alternative ruling body to the Crown.

Of the eight Scots-Irish signators, John Hancock from Massachusetts is undoubtedly the best known. He was the President of Congress and his signature on the Declaration was not only the first but the largest. It was reputed that King George III had bad eyesight and Hancock wrote large to make sure his name was not missed. On completing his signature, Hancock, of Banbridge, Co. Down extraction, said: "There, I guess King George will be able to read that".

The other seven known Scots-Irishmen who signed the famous document were:

• **William Whipple** - his parents had arrived in Maine from Ireland in 1730.

• **Robert Paine** - his grandfather came from Dungannon, Co.Tyrone.

• **Thomas McKean** - his father came from Ballymoney, Co. Antrim.

- **Thomas Nelson** - his grandfather came from Strabane, Co. Tyrone.
- **Matthew Thornton** - from Londonderry, he settled in New Hampshire in 1718.
- **George Taylor** - the son of an Ulster Presbyterian minister.
- **Edward Rutledge** - another son of an Ulster Presbyterian family.

After being transcribed, debated and signed by the Continental Congress, the Declaration was then passed on to another native-born Ulsterman for printing. John Dunlap had moved from a printing company in Strabane, Co. Tyrone to work in America in the mid-18th century and it fell on him the honour of printing the first copies of the Declaration. Later in 1784, Dunlap had the distinction of printing America's first daily newspaper, The Pennsylvania Packet. Soon after it was signed the Declaration was widely distributed throughout America, with the first public reading being enacted by Colonel John Nixon, whose father was also Ulster-born.

The first newspaper to publish the full text of the Declaration outside America was the Belfast News Letter, today Northern Ireland's leading morning newspaper and of which the author of this book is assistant editor. Details of the Declaration had arrived by ship from America in the port of Londonderry about six weeks after it was signed and it was taken the 100 miles to the offices of the Belfast News Letter, then published by brothers Henry and Robert Joy.

The news caused much stir in Belfast and for the News Letter, which also carries the distinction of today being the oldest newspaper in the English-speaking world, founded in 1737, it was a European scoop. King George III in London had not even been acquainted of the news of the Declaration - News Letter readers in Belfast were among the first to know on their side of the Atlantic. Later in its edition of September 6-10, 1776, the News Letter reported on the historic events in Philadelphia.

"The 4th of July, 1776, the Americans appointed as a day of fasting and prayer, preparatory to their dedicating their country to God, which was done in the following manner: 'The Congress being assembled after having declared America independent, they had a crown placed on a Bible, which by prayer and solemn devotion they offered to God. The religious ceremony being ended they divided the crown into 13 parts, each of the United Provinces taking a part'."

The News Letter had been an influential vehicle for relaying news of the migration of the Scots-Irish Presbyterians to America. The paper carried many advertisements for the passage to America, most of them making special provision for contracted labour in the new lands.

Conscious of the strong link between Ulster and the American colonies the paper kept its readers fully informed about developments affecting their kinsfolk across the Atlantic. The events leading up to and during the War of Independence were detailed and news of the crucial Battle of Kings Mountain in South Carolina on October 7, 1780 was reported in the Belfast News Letter of February 6, 1781.

It came in the form of a letter despatched from William Davison to General Jethro Sumner from Camp Rocky-river (October 12, 1780). William Davison was a lieutenant in the revolutionary army in the Kings Mountain battle, an Ulsterman of good Presbyterian stock.

The letter read: "Sir, I have the pleasure of handing you very agreeable intelligence from the West. Patrick Ferguson, the great partizan, has miscarried. This we are assured of by Mr. Tate, Brigade Major in General Sumner's late command; the particulars from this gentleman's mouth stand thus: that Colonels Campbell, Cleveland, Shelby, Sevier, Williams, Brandon, Lacey, etc formed a conjunct body near Gilbert Town consisting of 3,000. From this body were selected 1,600 good horsemen who immediately went in pursuit of Colonel Ferguson, who was making his way to Charlotte. Our people overtook him posted on Kings Mountain, and on the evening of 7th instant, at four o'clock, began the attack, which continued 47 minutes. Colonel Ferguson fell in the action beside 160 of his men; 810 were made prisoners, including the British; 150 of the prisoners are wounded: 1,500 stand of arms fell into our hands. Colonel Ferguson had about 1,400 men. Our people surrounded them and the enemy surrendered. We lost about 20 men, among them is Major Chonicle, of Lincoln County; Colonel Williams is mortally wounded. The number of our wounded cannot be ascertained. This blow will certainly affect the British considerably. The Brigade Major who gives this was in the action. The above is true. The blow is great. I give you joy upon the occasion".

12

Davy Crockett: *king of the wild frontier*

few Americans have been surrounded by legend and myth quite
like Davy Crockett - frontiersman, Indian and Mexican fighter,
bear hunter and politician. The stirring exploits of this colourful
and courageous character from the rural backwoods of north east
Tennessee were indeed for real along the frontier 200 years ago and
were of the kind that made America great.

David Crockett (he never called himself Davy) was not born on a
mountain top as the parody in the Hollywood movie would have us
believe. He was born in a humble log cabin in a valley alongside the
Big Limestone River and the Nolichuckey River in Greene County on
August 17, 1786.

This fifth child in a family of nine (six sons and three daughters) to
John and Rebecca Crockett had an adventurous spirit from an early age
and though the schooling he received was very basic he managed to
acquire enough education to take him to the Congress in Washington.
Davy Crockett was a man of the people on the frontier: a plain honest to
goodness backwoodsman, but with enough intelligence, common sense
and cunning to outwit even his most highly educated political opponents.

Sadly, Davy was only 49 when he died from a Mexican bullet at the
Alamo on March 6, 1836, but he was a man who had lived life to the
full and long before his tragic demise his heroics as a frontiersman were
the talk of the nation.

Davy's ancestors were Scots-Irish Presbyterians who had emigrated to America from counties Tyrone and Donegal in the north west part of Ulster. The family had (originally) been French Protestant Huguenots taking the name of Crocketagne in the 17th century and they moved to Ireland via England and Scotland during the plantation years.

The Crocketts settled in the region around the present-day towns of Castlederg (Co. Tyrone) and Donegal and several were involved in the Siege of Londonderry, defending the Williamite cause. They became related to the Stewarts of Donegal, when one of the first Crocketts to reach America's shores in the early 18th century, Joseph Louis, married Sarah Stewart.

Davy is a great grandson of William Crockett, a brother of Joseph Louis, and the family settled temporarily in Pennsylvania and Maryland about the mid-18th century, before later moving on to the Carolinas and Tennessee.

David Crockett, Davy's grandfather, passed through the Shenandoah valley in Virginia, verified by the fact that his son Robert was born at Berryville in the region in 1755. By 1771 the Crocketts had moved to North Carolina and deed records of Tryon (note the Irish sounding place name) confirm that he bought a 250-acre farm on the south side of the Catawbe River in that year.

Within a few years the family had moved further westwards to the Holston River valley and formed a settlement at Carter's Creek, where Rogersville in East Tennessee now stands. Soon this became known to many as Crockett's Creek and three of David Crockett's three sons - John, William and Joseph - had separate farmlands. Davy's father John had his three miles from David Sen's place.

In November, 1777, tragedy was to hit the family. The area was still a highly dangerous place with Cherokee tribes showing a lot of hostility towards the white settlers and it was while David Crockett, his wife and at least one other member of the family were putting in crops in the fields that the Indians struck. The elder Crocketts were brutally murdered and one of their sons was taken captive.

It was a massacre which had a chilling effect on the tightly-knit community of settlers, most of them Scots-Irish, and for them the stark message was either to organise a cohesive defensive strategy or die. Today a gravestone in the centre of Rogersville records the murders of David Crockett and his wife. Alongside it is the grave of Co. Tyrone man Joseph Rogers, who gave his name to Rogersville. The Crockett grave marker reads: "Here lies the bodies of David Crockett and his wife, grandparents of Davy Crockett, who were massacred within their cabin near this spot in the year 1777".

John Crockett and another brother Robert took part in the various Revolutionary War campaigns and both fought at the Battle of Kings Mountain in 1780, along with six other members of the connection. John married Rebecca Hawkins, who was born in Maryland and whose family too arrived in North Carolina via the valley of Virginia.

Soon after the death of his parents John Crockett moved his family to Limestone Creek in the neighbouring Greene County. It was the period when attempts were being made to form the separate state of Franklin on lands that were in North Carolina, but the new state collapsed and there is truth in the claim that Davy Crockett was born in North Carolina, even though today Limestone Creek is in Tennessee. A simple limestone slab on the site of his father's wooden cabin at Limestone, Greene County reads: "On this spot Davy Crockett was born August 17, 1786".

Davy Crockett spent only the first few years of his life in Limestone. The family moved to Cove Creek where his father had a partnership in a mill, but it was a short stay for the mill and the Crockett home was destroyed in a flood. The next stop was Jefferson County, Tennessee and John Crockett opened a tavern on the road from Abingdon to Knoxville.

Davy was only eight and stayed there until he was 12, when he was hired out as a cattle hand to a Dutch settler Jacob Siler in Rockville, Virginia. The employment was rewarding, but homesickness forced Davy to complete the 400-mile journey to his Tennessee frontier home. His father sent him to school, but he played truant after only four days and, fearing punishment at home, cut his family ties and decided to seek employment in the wider world.

For nearly three years Davy moved from job to job and, after passing through Virginia, he worked for a time at the docks in Baltimore. Still only 15, he returned home to find his father in debt to the amount of 86 dollars and gladly bound himself to work out for the sum involved.

While working for a Quaker, John Kennedy, Davy managed to gain the only educational experience he had in his life and the six months schooling provided him with the basics to advance his career. Davy was an adventurer, a hunter who lived off the land ... he was streetwise in the culture of the forests, the rivers and the mountains, as sharp as any of his peers on the frontier.

Marriage beckoned and after several romances he found a partner in pretty Polly Finley, who had Scots-Irish connections on her maternal side. They wed in 1806 despite the opposition of the girl's mother, who was looking for better than the restless backwoodsman Crockett.

Davy and Polly lived for a few years on a rented farm near her father's home in Jefferson County. But the going was hard and when two sons were born, John Wesley in 1807 and William in 1809, Davy decided it was time to seek more fertile land further west in middle Tennessee, beyond the Cumberland Mountains.

By the fall of 1811 the Crocketts had found the ideal place near the headwaters of Mulberry Creek, on the Duck and Elk Rivers in what is now Moore County, Tennessee. The surrounding forests were rich in deer and smaller game and it was there that Davy Crockett the hunter came into his own.

Within two years he moved the family to Bean Creek in Franklin County, to a home he called "Kentuck" and stayed there until after his involvement in Andrew Jackson's war with the Indians in 1812-14.

Crockett originally volunteered for 90-day service in the Second Regiment of Volunteer Mounted Riflemen, but the military duties were extended and he was selected as a scout to spy on the Creek Indian territory, along with a close friend George Russell. It was during these expeditions that Davy really gained the reputation of being a bear hunter, skilfully bearing the Kentucky long rifle.

Killing bears was something Davy had been proficient at since he was a boy. On a tree in Washington County, Tennessee there's a carving with the inscription: "Ciled bear DAVE CROCKETT 1796". Davy never was good at spelling.

He joined up with the regular army and battled with the Indians at Fort Strother and Fort Taladega and encountered British forces in the Florida campaign. Polly his wife, meanwhile, had taken ill back at Mulberry Creek and Davy had to return home. She was always a delicate, frail person and the many moves and natural hardships she faced in the frontier wilderness sapped her strength and energy.

She died in the summer of 1815, leaving Davy with three young children to care for - two boys and an infant daughter Margaret Polly. A distraught Davy - he loved Polly greatly - persuaded a younger brother and his wife to come and live with him to help look after the three small children.

Within a year Davy married again, to a widow Elizabeth Patton, the mother of two children whose husband had been killed in the Creek War. Elizabeth was a woman of good family background (North Carolina stock), who owned a sizeable farm and the marriage helped Davy to increase his status. She died in Texas in 1860, aged 72.

Davy, despite having taken on another wife and two more children, continued to explore and with neighbouring settlers he looked over the Alabama territory which had just been acquired from the Creek Indians. On that expedition, he contacted malaria and was fortunate to get home alive.

He took advantage of the treaty of 1816 with the Chickasaw Indians and found another settlement at Shoal Creek near Lawrenceburg in middle-Tennessee. Within two months, Davy was a justice of the peace and later became lieutenent colonel of the local militia. His new found civic and legal duties, on his own admission, were seriously taxing his educational ability, but he claimed that he got by on his "natural born sense", rather than any knowledge of the law.

He was elevated to colonel in the militia and in 1821 was elected to the Tennessee state legislature for Lawrence and Hickman counties. While electioneering he admitted he never read a newspaper and knew nothing about government, but he had talents as a soap box orator and a humour which endeared him to ordinary voters.

Crockett, gifted as a storyteller, was looked down on by representatives of the moneyed classes and slightingly referred to as "the gentleman from the cane", but he knew his frontier constituency and the poorer backwoods families rallied to his cause.

While attending the legislature at Murfreesborough his large grist, powder mill and distillery on Shoal Creek were swept away in a flood - a repeat of the misfortune which struck his father at Cove Creek - and he was forced to move the family to Rutherford Fork, 150 miles distance. He was re-elected to the legislature in 1823, defeating Dr. William E. Butler, a nephew of the wife of Andrew Jackson and one of the region's most wealthy men.

Butler had education, money and influence, Crockett the uncanny knack of persuading voters over on to his side. In his accounts, Davy tells of a special hunting shirt which he wore when campaigning. It was made of buckskin, outsize and had two pockets. In one pocket he carried whiskey and in the other tobacco. Davy reckoned that when he met a prospective voter he would treat him first with whiskey and before leaving him he would hand him a twist of tobacco to replace the "chaw" he had disposed off when he took the drink. The reasoning was that if a man was in good humour, in as good a shape as when he found him, the vote was secure on polling day. Butler was routed at the polls and Crockett returned to represent five counties.

Crockett was, in many respects, a socialist, although he espoused the capitalist free market ideals of the American dream. The major issue for the 1823 legislature was the disposition of lands belonging to the state and the mopping up of the territory formerly under the control of North Carolina. Crockett, joined by US President to be James K. Polk, figured prominently in this debate. He also opposed legislative handling of divorce cases and had numerous run-ins with Andrew Jackson, shortly to become President.

Davy had two terms as a state legislator and in 1825 he was setting his sights on a career in the American Congress. He was elected in 1827, defeating General William Arnold and Colonel Adam Alexander who had both foolishly ignored the Crockett bandwagon convinced it was a straight fight. The margin of victory was 2,748 votes and Davy went to the White House to represent West Tennessee, the region he had lived in since 1821.

He had two terms in Congress and it is generally thought he would have been elected for a third time had it not been for his opposition to Andrew Jackson's Indian Bill. On his stance over the Bill, Davy said: "I am at liberty to vote as my conscience and judgment dictate to be right, without the yoke of any party on me, or the driver at my heels, with the whip in his hands, commanding me 'gee-whoa-haw' just at his pleasure".

In whatever group Davy appeared he brought the flavour of the frontier. "Make way for Colonel Crockett," cried an usher at President Jackson's home one evening when the congressman from Tennessee presented himself. "Colonel Crockett makes room for himself," was his response as he strode confidently into the presence of the President.

It was during his last term in Congress that Davy made a trip to major eastern cities and New England states and wherever he went he was met by huge crowds and great ovations. He was in demand as a speaker at banquets and dinner parties and when he visited Philadelphia he was presented with the famous rifle "Betsy". This bore the gold and silver inscription: "To the honorable Davy Crockett of Tennessee by the young men of Philadelphia". "Betsy" was to accompany Davy on his last fateful journey - to Texas for the battles with the Mexicans - and nostalgically the trusted weapon was recovered by his family after the fall at the Alamo.

On November 1, 1835, three months after he was defeated in his third election to Congress, Davy Crockett left his West Tennessee home for Texas. His political career was over, the tremendous urge to explore new territory had again seized him - he was setting off to try and improve his economic well-being on the Texas frontier. "You can go to hell, I'm going to Texas," Davy told contemporaries.

He moved to Texas down the Mississippi River through Arkansas and into the Red River Valley. He was verging on Commanche Indian country where the tribes were on the warpath, as menacing to the American settlers as the Mexicans under their President Santa Anna.

Soon after his arrival Davy took the oath of allegiance to the provisional government of the independent republic of Texas. Another who took the oath at the time was his nephew William Patton, who had accompanied him to Texas in a party which was to become known as the "Tennessee Mounted Volunteers".

Texas was in revolt against the ruling junta in Mexico and the die was cast for a fight to the death. Crockett led the company of volunteers pledged to augment the defences at the Alamo, an old walled Franciscan mission station, where 185 men, together with some women, children and black servants had taken refuge from the advancing 5,000-strong Mexican army led by Santa Anna.

Most of the volunteers, including Crockett, were Tennesseans, the rest were Kentuckians and Virginians, and among the brave defenders at Alamo was another Tennessean of Scottish roots Colonel Jim Bowie, the man credited with inventing the Bowie knife. Illness from tuberculosis prevented Jim from taking an active role in the battle.

The station was under the command of Colonel William Travis, aged only 25, who kept repeating even in the face of the enemy: "Victory or death! I shall never surrender or retreat!" Sam Houston, like Crockett of Ulster-Scots extraction, was major-general of the regular army in the new independent republic to Texas, but it was an army which existed only on paper - it still had to be recruited. It looked ominous with Santa Anna and his army closing in, after occupying the nearby city of San Antonio. During the 12 days that Colonel Travis held the Alamo he fired guns at sunrise, which in the clear morning air, could be heard 100 miles across the plains. The gunfire was tragically to fall on deaf ears.

The siege began on February 23, 1836 and Crockett's pledge to Colonel Travis was: "Colonel, here I am. Assign me a position and I and my 12 boys will try to defend it". The "boys" were the Tennesseans and to the most vulnerable point at the station they were assigned.

Eighteen cannon were mounted as the siege began and Travis in his report said: "The Hon. David Crockett was seen at all points animating the men to do their duty". The accurate rifle fire of the Tennesseans kept the Mexicans at bay, but time and supplies were running out. And there was no sign of the army reinforcements that had been promised.

A detachment of 32 men managed to arrive on March 1, but two days later there came the news from a courier that 400 men had turned back because of difficulties on the way and because the officers felt another Texas station was more in need of defending than the Alamo.

Santa Anna decided that the fort should be taken by assault and the first two charges were beaten back with huge losses on the part of the Mexicans. In a third assault, concentrating on the north wall of the fort, Mexicans managed to breach the defences and gain access to the plaza of the mission.

It was a bleak situation, with the outnumbered Texans having to retreat to buildings around the plaza and the mission church, but the cannons were seized and used to batter down the doors. The defenders took their last stand in hand-to-hand combat and many finished at the receiving end of a Mexican bayonet.

An estimated 185 Texans were killed, with their bodies placed on a funeral pyre and burned. The only survivors were non-combatants, mostly Mexican women and children, several black slaves of Colonel Bowie and Colonel Travis and a Mrs. Dickinson, the wife of an officer of the garrison.

Various accounts of how Davy Crockett died at the Alamo have been put forward. It is claimed he was one of six survivors who surrendered to Santa Anna and was shot dead on the Mexican leader's orders. But it is generally accepted that he fell behind the south wall which he and the Tennesseans were charged to defend.

Mrs. Dickinson, who was led from the church, said in her testimony: "As we passed through the enclosed ground in front of the church I saw heaps of dead and dying. I recognised Colonel Crockett lying dead and mutilated between the church and the barrack building, and even remember seeing his peculiar cap lying by his side".

Two slave witnesses, Santa Anna's cook Ben and Colonel Travis's servant Joe, claimed Crockett's body was surrounded by Mexican corpses. Ben reported seeing Davy's knife buried "up to the hilt in the bosom of a Mexican found lying across his body".

For General Sam Houston, the fall of the Alamo was an agonising nightmare. Sam was presiding at a convention in Washington which was deliberating on the independence of Texas and when word reached him of the last message ever despatched by Colonel Travis he walked out, mounted his battle horse and with three companions headed for the Alamo.

The party rode hard all day and only stopped when their wearied horses could go no further. He knew that the signal gun would be fired as long as the Alamo held out. The last one was fired on the day that he had read Travis's message (Sunday March 6) - the day the Mexicans butchered 185 men. Sam Houston was too late to render assistance at the Alamo, but through his leadership, and against all the odds, he managed to retrieve the positon for the Texan cause in the days that followed.

The Alamo, by tieing down Santa Anna's army for two weeks, had allowed the Texan army to get organised. The battle cry had now become "Remember the Alamo" and, under Houston, the Texans, heavily outnumbered but determined to "save Texas", won a famous victory at the Battle of San Jacinto.

It was 700 brave but largely untrained Texans against 1,800 Mexicans, but buoyed by the frenzied cries of "The Alamo", Houston's men won the day in 20 minutes. The Mexicans had 630 killed and 730 prisoners were taken including Santa Anna. The Texan losses were eight killed and 23 injured.

Houston, who suffered an ankle injury in the battle, secured from Santa Anna a treaty recognising Texas independence and by September of that year he was President of the new republic. Texas later became a state of the Union - the 28th - on December 29, 1845.

On March 24, 1836 the Telegraph and Texas Register in Austin reported: "The end of Davy Crockett of Tennessee, the great hunter of the west, was as glorious as his career through life had been useful. He and his companions were found surrounded by piles of assailants, whom they had immolated on the altar of Texas liberties. The countenance of Crockett was unchanged: he had in death that freshness of hue, which his exercise of pursuing the beasts of the forest and the prairie had imparted to him. Texas places him, exultingly, amongst the martyrs of her cause".

Davy's son, John Wesley Crockett, who later represented his father's old constituency of West Tennessee in the American Congress, wrote to his uncle George Patton of North Carolina: "You have doubtless seen the account of my father's fall at the Alamo in Texas. He is gone from us and is no more to be seen in the walks of men, but in his death like Sampson (Samson) he slew more of his enemies than in all of his life. Even his most bitter enemies here, I believe, have buried all animosity and joined the great lamentation over his untimely death".

Davy's last reported memorandum, written on March 5, - the day he died, carried the words: "Pop, pop, pop, bom, bom! Throughout the day. No time for memorandums now. Go ahead! Liberty and independence forever!"

Some military strategists might look back on the Alamo as a blunder - that a body of soldiers were allowed to be surrounded by a force vastly superior in numbers, but it is widely accepted that the supreme sacrifice made by Davy Crockett and the others in the little mission station largely contributed to the securing of independence for Texas.

Shortly after the Alamo John Wesley Crockett went to Texas to retrieve his father's rifle "Betsy" and with other personal belongings the weapon became a treasured possession in the family, being handed down from generation to generation. David Crockett once wrote: "I'll leave this truth for others when I'm dead. First be sure you are right and then go ahead".

It is said Davy Crockett possessed the essential attributes for the American frontier. He was an adventurer, with a talent for falling in with strangers, a memory for names and faces, a gift of storytelling, inexhaustable invention, indomitable valiance, a remarkable ability for sharp-shooting and that freedom from conscience that springs from a contempt for pettiness and bureaucracy. He was a free soul who sought the company only of those of like temperament, a man in the highest traditions of his Scots-Irish heritage. The legend and myth of David Crockett was indeed real.

THE LONG RIFLE

The Kentucky long rifle was the weapon most favoured by the Scots-Irish settlers who pushed the American frontier westwards to the Mississippi and beyond. It was the weapon that opened up the west.

This muzzle-loading, flintlock firearm was modified from a short, large-bore rifle which was brought first to America by German and Swiss immigrants in the early 18th century. The German version was essentially a hunting rifle, with the bore installed with special grooves to make the bullet spin and travel more accurately.

In the American frontier such a weapon was needed to hunt and to defend oneself, family and stock from attack. The rifle had to be durable, dependable, accurate and with a capacity for constant fire. Gunsmiths got to work and the most significant change from the original German concept was a lengthening of the barrel to improve accuracy and range. Increasing the length burned more of the gunpowder before the ball left the bore and this added pressure reached to a longer target. The calibre of the rifle was also reduced from .75 down to between .35 and .50 which allowed for more shots from a pound of gunpowder.

When the movement into the Appalachians began in earnest, about the mid-18th century, the art of gunsmithing expanded and in most mountain settlements there was a man who made a living assembling long rifles for his pioneering friends.

Materials for these firearms were easy to find in places like Virginia, Kentucky, the Carolinas and Tennessee: walnut and maple trees produced the stocks; local mines the lead for the bullets; steel for the springs came from worn-out saws and files. Only the gunpowder had to be imported.

In the Smoky Mountains of East Tennessee the uses of a gun fell into different categories: a squirrel gun was .35 calibre; a turkey gun .40 calibre; a deer gun .45 calibre and a bear gun .50 calibre. The long rifle was the constant companion of the frontiersman, as he defended his homeland from the ravages of wild animals and from Indian attack. It was seldom, however, used by armies in battle, mainly because it was slow to load, was less effective than a musket, more expensive to produce and could not be fitted with a bayonet.

American revolutionaries, however, used the long rifle to good effect in the battles with the British and the Indians and it was at Kings Mountain in South Carolina on October 7, 1780 that the weapon came into its own.

The Overmountain Men, a force made up mostly of Scots-Irish settlers, routed an 1,100-strong contingent of Redcoats, commanded by Colonel Patrick Ferguson, with long rifles. The 910 riflemen, using the wooded terrain for cover, took an hour to gain the most significant victory in the Revolutionary War. Ferguson and 225 of his men were killed; 163 were wounded - the rest were taken captive. Only 28 of the mountain men were killed and 62 wounded.

Later in 1814, General Andrew Jackson's Tennesseans used the long rifles to defeat the Creek Indians at Horseshoe Bend in Alabama and in 1815 the riflemen again saw action, under Jackson, at the Battle of New Orleans. The British had 2,000 casualties - the Americans amazingly only seven killed and six wounded.

The battle had been won by the wonderful marksmanship of the Kentucky and Tennessee riflemen - the Scots-Irish. The long-barrelled weapon which wielded such considerable influence in the south-west frontier states was aptly named "the instrument of destiny".

13

Sam Houston: *luminary of Tennessee and Texas*

S am Houston - the grandson of an Ulster Presbyterian - was one of the leading American personalities of the 19th century, the man who wrested Texas from Mexican control to eventually become a state of the Union. From teacher to lawyer, soldier to statesman, Sam Houston made an indelible mark in the frontier regions and, although not universally acclaimed in his day, he led from the front in any of the assignments he tackled.

Sam (he preferred the name Samuel) was born in Timber Ridge, Rockbridge County, Virginia on March 2, 1793 about seven miles from the town of Lexington. His father Major Sam Houston was a veteran of the Revolutionary War who continued soldiering into the 19th century and who died in 1807 while on a tour inspection of frontier army posts.

The Houston (Huston) family connection can be traced back to the Ballyboley/Ballynure/Brackbracken area of East County Antrim in the north of Ireland - a plantation family who had moved from Scotland in the early 17th century.

In 1729, a famine year for the Scots settlers due to bad weather, there was a widow on a small farm of 25 acres in the townland of Ballybracken called Jane Houston. She had four sons aged between three and 12 and found, in spite of assistance by her neighbours, that she could not pay the rent of the farm to the landlord. Leases had run out in 1725 and were renewed with up to a sixth rise. These were years of very low yields and subsequent high prices with the result that scarcely any farmer had surplus to sell and in many cases had to use for food the oats and potatoes which should have been stored for seed.

The widow Houston decided that she could not carry on, in spite of the landlord's agent not pushing for money, and she gave up her tenancy. Under an unwritten law, applying only to the Province of Ulster, called Tenant Right, she was entitled on giving up her tenancy to reimbursement for improvements carried out during her tenancy. Her late husband had been an industrious worker.

With whatever money she received from her animals and chattels and the landlord she set off on foot to the port of Larne, contacting an emigration agent for North America and paying passage money for herself and her four sons to New York.

There is no record of her name for that year in the passenger lists from Larne and nothing is known of the time it took to cross the Atlantic or the hardships endured. A few lines by Ballynure's weaver poet, James Campbell (1756-1818), about another immigrant much later would adequately describe Mrs. Houston's feelings as she sailed for the open sea.

"Away tae the States frae the Port o' Larne
She sailed oot ower the sea
Like an autumn leaf on the river's drift
Torn from its native tree."

Mrs. Houston married again in New York. The four sons were reared to manhood and like the majority of the Ulster-Scots moved west and south as pioneers, ready to endure any hardship or hostile Red Indian in the quest for land.

John Huston, Sam Houston's grandfather, emigrated about 1740 and with other Presbyterian kinsfolk from Co. Antrim he settled in the valley of Virginia. The part of Co. Antrim where the Hustons lived was only a few miles from where the forebears of Major John Donelson, one of the founders of Nashville, and his son-in-law President Andrew Jackson resided. The Jackson and the Donelson families left the port of Larne for Philadelphia and it is believed the Hustons covered the same tracks. On arrival in America the family surname changed to Houston.

Religion played an important part in the lives of the early Houstons in America and it was the Presbyterian faith which had been taken from

James Knox Polk, the 11th President of the United States.
His family originated in Londonderry/Donegal

Columbia (Maury County, Tennessee), the mule capital of the world. Mule Day on the first week-end of April each year, attracts hundreds of thousands of people from across America. Columbia was an early Scots-Irish settlement in Tennessee.

Hale Springs Inn at Rogersville, Tennessee - built in 1824 by Coleraine (Northern Ireland) man John Augustine McKinney.

The Knoxville site of Fort Adair, built in 1788 by Co. Antrim-born John Adair, the man who raised the money for the Revolutionary soldiers at the Battle of Kings Mountain in 1780.

Boneybefore at Carrickfergus, Co. Antrim - the site of the ancestral home of President Andrew Jackson.

Shiloh Presbyterian Church, outside Gallatin in middle Tennessee, founded by Scots-Irish settlers in 1793

Memorial at Larne Harbour to the first Ulster emigrants who sailed to America in 1717.

viii

Joseph Rogers, the Cookstown, Co. Tyrone man, who founded the town of Rogersville in East Tennessee, with his wife Mary Amis.

Lebanon in the Fork, near Knoxville, site of a Presbyterian Church founded by Scots-Irish in 1791.

*John Augustine McKinney, from Coleraine, Co. Londonderry, who was a
leading lawyer in East Tennessee in the early 19th century.*

Andrew Johnson, the American President of Larne, Co. Antrim roots.

Anno 1776.] HENRY AND ROBERT JOY. [Numb. 4075

The BELFAST NEWS-LETTER.

From FRIDAY AUGUST 23, to TUESDAY AUGUST 27, 1776.

[Remainder of the last PACKETS.]

AMERICA.

In CONGRESS, JULY 4, 1776.

A DECLARATION by the REPRESENTATIVES of the UNITED STATES of AMERICA, in GENERAL CONGRESS assembled.

WHEN in the course of human events it becomes necessary for one people to dissolve the political bands which have connected them with another, and to assume among the powers of the earth the separate and equal station to which the laws of nature and of nature's God entitle them, a decent respect to the opinions of mankind requires that they should declare the causes which impel them to the separation.

We hold these truths to be self-evident; that all men are created equal; that they are endowed by their Creator with certain unalienable rights; that among these are life, liberty, and the pursuit of happiness. That to secure these rights, governments are instituted among men, deriving their just powers from the consent of the governed; and whenever any form of government becomes destructive of these ends, it is the right of the people to alter or to abolish it, and to institute new government, laying its foundation on such principles, and organizing its powers in such form, as to them shall seem most likely to effect their safety and happiness. Prudence indeed will dictate, that governments long established should not be changed for light and transient causes; and accordingly all experience hath shewn, that mankind are more disposed to suffer, while evils are sufferable, than to right themselves by abolishing the forms to which they are accustomed. But when a long train of abuses and usurpations, pursuing invariably the same object, evinces a design to reduce them under absolute despotism, it is their right, it is their duty, to throw off such government, and to provide new guards for their future security. Such has been the patient sufferance of these Colonies, and such is now the necessity which constrains them to alter their former systems of government. The history of the present King of Great-Britain, is a history of repeated injuries and usurpations; all having in direct object the establishment of an absolute tyranny over these States. To prove this, let facts be submitted to a candid world.

He has refused his assent to laws, the most wholesome and necessary for the public good.

He has forbidden his Governours to pass laws of immediate and pressing importance, unless suspended in their operation till his assent should be obtained; and when so suspended, he has utterly neglected to attend to them.

He has refused to pass other laws for the accommodation of large districts of people; unless those people would relinquish the rights of representation in the legislature, a right inestimable to them, and formidable to tyrants only.

He has called together legislative bodies at places unusual, uncomfortable, and distant from the depository of their public records, for the sole purpose of fatiguing them into compliance with his measures.

He has dissolved representative houses repeatedly, for opposing, with manly firmness, his invasions on the rights of the people.

[illegible]

with circumstances of cruelty and perfidy, scarcely paralleled in the most barbarous ages, and totally unworthy the head of a civilized nation.

He has constrained our fellow citizens, taken captive on the High Seas, to bear arms against their country, to become the executioners of their friends and brethren, or to fall themselves by their hands.

He has excited domestic insurrections amongst us, and has endeavoured to bring on the inhabitants of our frontiers, the merciless Indian Savages, whose known rule of warfare is an undistinguished destruction of all ages, sexes, and conditions.

In every stage of these oppressions we have petitioned for redress, in the most humble terms; our repeated petitions have been answered only by repeated injury.—A Prince, whose character is thus marked by every act which may define a tyrant, is unfit to be the ruler of a free people.

Nor have we been wanting in attention to our British brethren. We have warned them, from time to time, of attempts, by their legislature, to extend an unwarrantable jurisdiction over us. We have reminded them of the circumstances of our emigration and settlement here. We have appealed to their native justice and magnanimity, and we have conjured them by the ties of our common kindred to disavow these usurpations which would inevitably interrupt our connections and correspondence. They too have been deaf to the voice of justice and of consanguinity. We must, therefore, acquiesce in the necessity which denounces our separation, and hold them, as we hold the rest of mankind, enemies in war, in peace friends.

We, therefore, the Representatives of the United States of America, in General Congress assembled, appealing to the supreme judge of the world for the rectitude of our intentions, do, in the name and by the authority of the good people of these Colonies, solemnly publish and declare, that these United Colonies are, and of right ought to be, FREE AND INDEPENDENT STATES, and that they are absolved from all allegiance to the British Crown, and that all political connection between them and the State of Great-Britain, is and ought to be totally dissolved; and that as free and independent States, they have full power to levy war, conclude peace, contract alliances, establish commerce, and to do all other acts and things which independent States may of right do. And for the support of this Declaration, with a firm reliance on the protection of Divine Providence, we mutually pledge to each other our lives, our fortunes, and our sacred honour.

Signed by Order, and in Behalf of the Congress.

JOHN HANCOCK, President.

Attest. CHARLES THOMSON, Secretary.

LONDON, Aug. 16.

Extract of a letter from an officer in the 35th regiment, at Staten Island, dated July 9, 1776.

"On the 4th inst. we landed on this island, and are in very comfortable cantonments amongst a loyal and liberal people, who produce us in plenty, and in agreeable variety, all the necessaries of life; most of which we had long been deprived of during our late service in the Eastern provinces. Our army consisted of six thousand one hundred and fifty-five effectives, on our embarkation at Halifax; they are now all safe landed [illegible] and our head quarters at your late old

Orange county; but our old friends and countrymen Hugh and Alexander Wallace, together with those two chearful Englishmen Wallace and Sherbrook, after having got over to Long Island, have not yet been able to reach our camp. Poor Charles Evers has been long missing; he fled into the woods, and has never since been heard of. The Provincials have driven most of the cattle from Long Island to the Island of New York; they were employed in carrying off all that existed on Staten Island, but luckily were prevented by the critical arrival of our troops.

"The New York papers tells us that the dull, verbose Donald Cambell, who had long prevailed at the head of the New York mobs, insulting and torturing the friends of government, has been tried and dismissed the Provincial service, for his two late alert retreats in the Province of Quebec. His Majesty's half-pay list I find has been lately exonerated of this caitiff. We are just now informed that the lady and family of Sir John Johnson have been taken prisoners by the splendid, and hitherto invincible General Schuyler, by way of hostages, for Sir John is at the head of a number of the six Indian nations, and on his way to facilitate the progress of the British troops from Canada to Albany, &c.——So much, my dear fellow soldier, for narrative; my next may produce a detail of a more active kind.

"The troops in these cantonments have just such an appearance as those dispatched by Sir Jeffery against Martinico and the Havannah; there is not an invalid nor a single noneffective in our army; we expect orders to land the army beyond the King's bridge, and make our approach to the city on the rear of the island, in which case Mr. Washington must present his front to us in the fair field, or submit to an alternative which in its event, will put an end this hurlyburly touching independence."

Letters from Virginia, by the way of Glasgow, give an account of an engagement between the Liverpool frigate, of 28 guns, nine pounders, and a hundred and sixty men, and the Defiance and Revenge, two American privateers, the former of eighteen guns, six pounders, and one hundred and ten men, the latter of twelve guns, six and three pounders, and eighty men, in which the two privateers were torn almost to pieces; and on the Liverpool's tender (a brig) coming up, they both struck, supposing her to have been a sloop of war, but indeed they were in no condition to have got away, having neither brace or bow-line left, and seven and forty men killed, and a great number wounded. The action lasted upwards of two hours, during which they were always within point blank of each other, and no sea running—The guns of the Liverpool were exceedingly well served, and nothing could be worse than the gunners aboard the privateers, which accounts for the Liverpool having received but little damage, and only one man killed and seven wounded. The above action happened about ten leagues to the northward of Cape Fear.

NEW BOOKS.

This Day were published, and to be sold by JOHN HAY, junior, Bookseller, Belfast.

[Price, Two British Shillings, sewed in Marble Paper.]

1. A VIEW of the INTERNAL EVIDENCE of the CHRISTIAN RELIGION.

By SOAME JENYNS, Esq.

☞ The Demand for this Publication in England [illegible]

THE Attendance of the Linen Drapers of the County Tyrone, are requested at James Frost's of Dungannon, on Thursday the 29th Day of August, on particular Business.

TO be sold by Auction, at Bloomfield near Belfast, on Saturday the 31st August inst. for ready Money, fifteen Cocks of exceeding good well-saved Hay, and four Acres of good Oats on the Foot. August 22, 1776.

AN experienced, compleat Book-keeper, and Accomptant, that can be very well recommended for Sobriety and Honesty, would engage with a Merchant or Gentleman, as such. None need enquire of the Printer but those who will give a genteel Salary.

LOST,

ON Tuesday the 6th Inst. a small white Point Bitch; has a Liver-coloured Spot on the Crown of her Head, answers to the Name of Phillis. Whoever returns her, or informs Charles Duffen, Esq; of Dungannon, where she may be found, shall receive one Guinea Reward, and no Questions asked.

Dungannon, August 14th, 1776.

ADVERTISEMENT.

TO be sold by Auction, the Interest of a Lease now in Possession of Robert Mc. Clelland, in Cookstown, held under William Stewart, Esq; of Killymoon, for 3 Lives and 31 Years; a House 63 Feet long, two Stories high, with a large Shop, Kitchen, and Parlour, and a large Cellar under; and another Apartment belonging to said House, consisting of a Kitchen and two Rooms, all below Stairs, a large Dining-Room above the Shop, and five or six large Rooms above Stairs, a large Kitchen Garden, with six Acres and three Rood of Land convenient to the Town, well ditched and quicked, at the yearly Rent of 4l. 8s. per Year: This Place is suitable to a Shopkeeper, Tanner, Distiller, or Soap-boiler, as there is Plenty of Bog and Water; or a Linen Draper, as it is so convenient, eight Miles from Dungannon, four of Stewartstown, four of Cough, seven of Magherafelt, nine of Castle-dawson, all good Market Towns; also some Houshold Furniture, all to be sold Wednesday the 4th of September. Dated Cookstown, 13th August, 1776.

For ready Money,

TO be sold by publick Auction, on Friday the 30th Inst. at James Cooper's Coffee-House, Belfast, the whole Interest of the Lease of the Greeden Mill, and 12 Acres of Land, situate in the Parish of Killead, in the County of Antrim. There are fourteen Years of the Lease to come from November next, and three young Lives all in being, the Property of Mr. Thomas Potter of Bellow, in the County of Down.

N. B. There is ten Acres of said Farm set to a solvent Tenant, at the yearly Rent of 7l. 10s. during the Term of Years only; the whole is subject to the yearly Rent of 35 l. payable to Rowley Heyland, Esq; James Potter, of Mount-potter, in the County of Down [illegible] Person inclinable to purchase; and James Cunningham of Aughnamullen, will shew the Premisses.

[illegible] Dated August 19th, 1776.

N. B. The Cant to begin at 12 o'Clock.

THE Trustees appointed by Act of Parliament for executing the Turnpike Act between Banbridge and Randalstown, have appointed Monday the 2d Day of September next, to meet in the Market-House in Moira, to sell by Auction the Gates on the southern Division of said Act, to the highest and fairest Bidders, the Purchasers producing good Security. Dated August the 9th, 1776.

Signed by Order.

The August 23-27, 1776 edition of the Belfast News Letter announcing the news that the American Declaration of Independence had been signed on July 4, 1776

The inside of Zion Presbyterian Church at Columbia,
Maury County, Tennessee.

The original communion cups and chattels of Zion Presbyterian Church at
Columbia, Maury County, Tennessee, which was formed in 1809 by families
from Drumbo and Knockbracken outside Belfast.

*John Rhea, son of the
Rev. Joseph Rhea, the
minister of Fahan and
Innis Presbyterian
Churches in Co.
Donegal who moved to
America in 1769. John
Rhea, born in
Londonderry, became
a leading Tennessee
civic leader.*

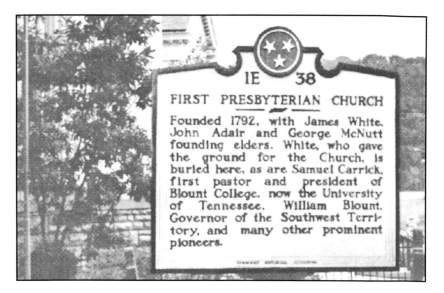

*The First Knoxville Presbyterian Church, founded in 1792 by Ulster-Scots
James White, John Adair, and George McNutt. The Rev. Samuel Carrick,
another of Scots-Irish descent, was the Church's first minister.*

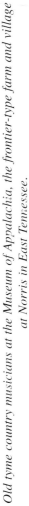

Old tyme country musicians at the Museum of Appalachia, the frontier-type farm and village at Norris in East Tennessee.

xiv

A stone fence at Scottsville Pike, Gallatin, Tennessee, similar to fences erected in Ulster and Scotland.

IN MEMORIAM
JAMES WHITE
FOUNDER OF KNOXVILLE
BORN-IREDELL COUNTY, N.C. 1747
DIED-KNOXVILLE, TENNESSEE, AUG. 14, 1821
CAPTAIN AND COLONEL IN
REVOLUTIONARY WAR
BRIGADIER GENERAL STATE TROOPS
ELDER FIRST PRESBYTERIAN CHURCH
DONOR OF LAND FOR THIS
CHURCH AND GRAVEYARD

ERECTED BY
JAMES WHITE'S CHAPTER
NATIONAL SOCIETY
DAUGHTERS OF
THE AMERICAN REVOLUTION
1942

The memorial tombstone of James White in the cemetery of First Knoxville Presbyterian Church.

Sam Houston, Governor of Tennessee and Texas - a man of East Antrim roots.

Matthew Rhea (1796-1870), grandson of the Rev. Joseph Rhea, and his wife Mary Looney.

The rally of the Overmountain people at Sycamore Shoals on September 25, 1780 prior to the Battle of Kings Mountain. The painting was completed in 1915 by Lloyd Branson, and presently hangs in the Tennessee State Museum in Nashville.

Scotland a century before that provided the cornerstone for these hardy frontier families.

The Houston family tree contains a long line of Presbyterian ministers and elders. John Houston founded the Providence Presbyterian Church at Rockbridge County in 1746 and he and his brother Sam often held prayer meetings in their own homes.

Major James Houston, a nephew of John Houston, was an elder of Maryville Presbyterian in Tennessee and six of his daughters married church ministers. Another pastor in the family was the Rev. Samuel Houston, a cousin of Sam, and his son the Rev. Samuel Rutherford Houston was a missionary to Greece. The Rev. Samuel Doak, who ministered to the Overmountain Men before they engaged in the Battle of Kings Mountain in 1780, was also of the Houston clan.

Sam's mother, Elizabeth Paxton Houston, was a devout Presbyterian who according to records of the time was "gifted with intellectual and moral qualities" above that of most women in the frontier. It was said her life was characterised by "purity and benevolence".

When her husband died she moved with her nine children - six sons and three daughters - from Virginia in the covered wagons to Maryville, Blount County in Tennessee. There she joined the Baker's Creek Presbyterian Church and twice and often three times a week she and the children walked the four miles over the hills to worship.

It was in this environment that Sam Houston grew up, his mother's Christian counselling an obvious influence to him. Later Sam admitted that the early impressions passed on from his mother far outlived all the wisdom of later life.

Sam really adored his mother. "Sages may reason and philosophers may teach, but the voice which we heard in infancy will ever come to our ears, bearing a mother's words and a mother's counsels", said Sam, who in his chequered career did not always live up to the Christian principles. He did, however, end his days as a Baptist convert.

When their father died, Sam and his brothers helped their mother erect the home at Maryville, at a point close to a river which divided the settlements of the pioneers from the lands of the Cherokee Indians.

Houston's early education was basic and when he was 16 he was apprenticed to a village store. But Sam was an adventurer and he became so attracted to the Cherokee Indian ways that he cut himself off from his family and went to live with the tribes for two years.

The Indian chief Oolooteka, known as "John Jolly", befriended Sam, who was given the title "The Raven". Sam adopted their dress and customs and mastered the Cherokee language, considered to be one of the most difficult in the world. The Indian sojourn earned Sam reproachment from his brothers for deserting the family, but, although he tired of the Indian ways, it was not to be the last time he aligned himself with the Cherokees.

Though Sam Houston had been in school for no more than six months of his first 13 years he was a self-taught student, who, amazingly for one brought up in the virtual wilderness of the frontier, delved into Greek and Roman history. When he ran away to live with the Cherokees he took with him a copy of Pope's translation of Iliad, which he used as the foundation of his learning.

When he was 18, Sam began teaching in a small country school in Tennessee. It was said that while Houston did not know much, his students knew less, so everything functioned in a satisfactory manner. From the school house Sam moved, at the age of 20 in 1813, to the army and after enlisting in the 7th United States Infantry he saw action in the war with the Creek Indians. He came to the notice of Andrew Jackson and within a year was promoted to sergeant and then to second lieutenant.

Sam was injured twice at the battle of To-ho-pe-ka in 1814; first with a barbed arrow through the eye and second when two rifle balls struck him on the shoulder. He was given up for dead, but managed to return home where his mother nursed him back to full health.

Jackson used Houston to cultivate relations with the Cherokees and his knowledge of the Indian language and culture enabled him to avert a threatened uprising by tribesmen after the chiefs had surrendered a vast amount of land to the United States. He later led a Cherokee delegation to Washington to receive payment for their lands and to settle on the bounds of their reservation.

By March, 1818, Sam was a first lieutenant, but by this time he had become disillusioned with the army over allegations of complicity in smuggling black slaves into the United States. He resigned his commission and was later vindicated in a Washington inquiry.

The next move for Sam was to Nashville, where he studied law and was admitted to the bar. In turn he was appointed a district attorney, an adjutant general for the state of Tennessee and major-general. This all proved to be a stepping stone for a career in politics and he was elected to the United States Congress in 1823, and re-elected in 1825.

Andrew Jackson was Houston's political mentor and it is recorded that in his four years in Congress Sam displayed "remarkable qualities of statesmanship". Sam was elected Governor of Tennessee in 1827, and was re-elected in 1829. Until then Sam had no serious relationships with women and it was not until he was 35 and Governor of Tennessee that he married the 18-year-old Eliza Allen, a young woman of position and character. The Presbyterian wedding was a lavish affair in terms of style and pageantry, but the couple only lived together for three months and Sam, resigning his position as Governor, disappeared back to the forests with the Cherokee Indians.

The break-up of the marriage caused uproar in Nashville, but Sam was unconcerned. The Cherokees had been moved to Oklahoma and Chief John Jolly (Oolooteka) welcomed Houston back as a son and gave him a certificate of adoption into the Cherokee tribe. Once again Sam took on the dress, customs and manners of the Cherokees and hunted, fished, attended war councils and, in keeping with the tribesmen, drank to excess, earning him the ignominious title of "Big Drunk".

During his three years with the Indians, Houston visited Washington several times on their behalf and, dressed in his Indian garb, he was warmly welcomed by President Jackson. He also cohabited with a half-breed Indian woman Tyania Rodgers Gentry and it was said he left her only when she refused to desert her people. His own wife later obtained a divorce for abandonment and re-married.

Texas was calling and in 1833 Sam headed to the Rio Grande country where a revolution was being planned to overthrow Mexican rule. He was welcomed by the American colonists at Nacogdoches and took part in talks with Comanche Indian chiefs on disputed boundary questions in the San Antonio region. The welfare of the Indians remained Sam's main concern.

Houston was in the vanguard of the independence movement and he sat on the convention at San Felipe de Austin which set in train the breakaway from Mexico. He was sworn in as major-general and commander-in-chief of the new revolutionary army, but time was not on his side - Mexican President Santa Anna was closing in with 5,000 men in three columns.

The Mexicans reached San Antonio and laid siege on The Alamo, an old walled Franciscan mission where 185 Texans and a collection of women, children and black slaves were holed up. Defending the fort were two old associates of Houston - Tennessean frontiersman Davy Crockett and Colonel Jim Bowie, but the situation was impossible and before reinforcements could be sent all able-bodied men at the station were killed.

The Alamo stirred Houston for action and he managed to recruit enough men - just over 700 - in the Texas auxiliaries to confront Santa Anna at the Battle of San Jacinto. The Texans were heavily outnumbered - there were 1,800 Mexicans, but in 20 minutes Houston's men, charging to the cry "Remember the Alamo", were victorious. The Mexicans lost 630 killed and had 730 taken prisoner, among them Santa Anna, and within a short time the Mexican President had given his consent to independence for Texas. Houston, injured in the ankle in the battle, became the first president of the new republic.

In May, 1840 Houston, then aged 47, married Margaret Lea, of Marion, Alabama and they had a happy stable relationship which produced eight children. Margaret was the daughter of a Baptist pastor and it was her influence which led to Sam's conversion at Independence, Texas in 1854.

From being a solid Presbyterian, Houston had experienced the heathen faiths of the Cherokees and flirted with Roman Catholicism. His espousal of the Baptist creed meant he had now come full circle.

It was while he was in Nacogdoches, Texas in 1833-34 that Sam joined the Roman Catholic Church. Texas at that time was under Mexican rule and anyone becoming a citizen had to be a Roman Catholic. Whether out of expediency or a willingness to dabble in the mysteries of another faith, Houston was baptised as a Roman Catholic and he chose the name Paul.

However, the fervour for his new religion waned and within a short period he was at odds with the Papacy and its influence on life in the Texas/Mexico territory. Urging his men to fight Mexico and criticising her arbitrary power, Houston declared: "Our constitutions have been declared at an end while all that is sacred is menaced by arbitrary power. The priesthood and the army are to mete out the measure of our wretchedness. Our only ambition is the attainment of national liberty - the freedom of religious opinion and just laws".

Towards the end of his life Sam Houston became very anti-Roman Catholic in his association with the Know-Nothing Party. The Know-Nothings were bitterly opposed to Roman Catholicism and foreigners who were gaining positions in the Democratic Party and Government and for a while Houston articulated their prejudices. This was paradoxical for Houston had, for most of his life, been a very tolerant man. The Know-Nothing phase for Sam lasted only a short period.

Houston had retired as President of Texas in 1844 and in March, 1846 he was elected as Senator to Washington from the Lone Star state. Texas had been admitted as a state of the Union on December 29, 1845 and Houston served for 14 years as a senator. During his senatorship he opposed the Southern doctrine that Congress had no right to legislate on slavery in the territories and he advocated California as a state of the Union and the development of the Pacific railroad through Texas.

In 1859 Sam was elected Governor of Texas as an Independent and served until March, 1861, when, on the enrolment of the state as a member of the Confederacy, he refused to take the necessary official oath and recognise the authority of the new convention. He was forced out of office by the Confederate politicians.

By now an old man, Houston was war-weary and did not resist. He wanted no more blood spilt among his own people. Sam retired to his farm at Huntsville and after an illness of five weeks he died on July 26, 1863, aged 70, as the Civil War was in progress.

For most of his life Sam Houston had been a prolific letter writer and after his conversion to the Baptist faith he regularly corresponded with his wife when away from home, giving resumes of sermons he had heard preached. Just before his conversion he became a member of the Sons of Temperance, but spurned a request from a delegation of Texas ministers who asked him to use his influence in getting a Sunday alcohol prohibition law passed. After outlining his reasons, Sam added: "I am a sincere Christian. I believe in the precepts and examples as taught and practised by Christ and His Apostles to be the bedrock of democracy". He often referred to his wife Margaret as being "one of the best Christians on earth".

One newspaper report of Sam's death said: "To his numerous friends it will be doubtless a matter of great satisfaction to learn that in his last hours he was sustained by the Christian's hope and that he died the death of the righteous".

Sam Houston was indeed a man of many parts. American historian Ernest C. Shearer accurately described his moods: "He was as inconstant as a weather vane, solid as a rock, mercurial as a chameleon, intense as the heat of the sun, enthusiastic as a child, vain and proud as a peacock, humble as a servant, direct as an arrow, polished as a marquis, rough as a blizzard and gentle as a dove. In short, it was difficult to fit him to any set pattern".

A few days before Sam died he made his will, and, in the fifth clause, he said: "To my eldest son, Sam Houston, I bequeath my sword, worn in the battle of San Jacinto, to be drawn only in defense of the constitution, and laws, and liberties of his country. If any attempt be made to assail one of these, I wish it to be used in its vindication".

The Civil War had already begun and Sam Jun., then only 20, was a Confederate soldier and, much to Sam Houston's regret, the American states were at each other's throats.

It was American President John F. Kennedy, who said of Sam Houston: "He was one of the most independent, unique, popular, forceful and dramatic individuals ever to enter the Senate Chamber. He was in turn magnanimous, vindictive, affectionate yet cruel, eccentric yet self-conscious, faithful yet opportunistic. But Sam Houston's contradictions actually confirm his one basic consistent quality: indomitable individualism, sometimes spectacular, sometimes crude, sometimes mysterious, but always courageous".

Sam's courage was no doubt fired by the unique Scots-Irish characteristic that tamed the frontier.

14

Links *that can be traced back to Drumbo*

A Presbyterian church in middle Tennessee can trace its origins directly back to a group of Ulster settlers who left Drumbo and Knockbracken in Co. Down for America during the early 18th century.

The present-day congregation of Zion Presbyterian Church near Columbia in Maury County, Tennessee is extremely proud of its Scots-Irish extraction and the witness being observed there is akin to that practised by the Reformed Presbyterian Church in Ireland, a denomination known as The Covenanters.

Zion Church's development was not without controversy, for it was after a congregational split that members moved from Williamsburg in South Carolina to middle Tennessee. Descendants of the Drumbo and Knockbracken families who are now connected with the Zion Church left the Lagan Valley in the north of Ireland for America about 1732-34 and after landing at Charleston they settled at Williamsburg, named in honour of King William, Prince of Orange who ascended to the English throne for the Protestant cause in 1688.

The settlers included the Witherspoons, Armstrongs, Wilsons and Friersons, families who, for almost 50 years, were to become known in South Carolina records as "the poor Protestants". In the first year of their settlement they were given provisions by the Council of South

Carolina. These included Indian corn, rice, wheat, flour, beef, pork, rum and salt. Each hand over 16 years of age was furnished with an axe and a broad and narrow hoe - tools of the land.

One of the settlers, weaver John Witherspoon was a relative of Dr. John Witherspoon, of New Jersey, who signed the American Declaration of Independence on July 4, 1776 and became president of Princeton College.

The Williamsburg John Witherspoon was said to be a man "well-versed" in the scriptures and the principles of Presbyterianism. Not surprisingly, considering his Ulster-Scots background of the mid-18th century, he had a great aversion to the Episcopacy.

The inhospitable land where they settled was virtually a timbered wilderness, infested with howling wolves and peopled by Indian tribes. Disease often decimated their numbers - in the great influenza epidemic known as the 'Great Mortality' 80 residents of the Williamsburg township perished. But they were a people undeterred.

Civil and religious liberty was the watchword of the Scots-Irish Presbyterians and, paradoxically, considering the pro-British attitudes of the Presbyterian community in Northern Ireland today, they were in the thrust of the American Revolution to sever the connections with Britain. The British looked upon all Presbyterian churches as "sedition houses" and this hostility caused deep resentment and bitterness among the settlers, who had left Ireland largely because of the intransigence of an Episcopalian-dominated regime.

In South Carolina for a period in the Revolutionary War the British forces were in the ascendancy, but they found the Scots-Irish extremely difficult to subdue. The countryside around Williamsburg was invaded several times by the Redcoats; Presbyterian churches and the homes of patriot members were burned.

The families at Williamsburg made a significant contribution to the Revolutionary War effort - William Frierson, in particular, had five sons who served as soldiers, with one, Major John Frierson, recorded for gallantry in the War Department at Washington.

The Williamsburg settlers were among the first wave of hardy Ulster settlers to arrive in the Americas and in 1736 they were given two acres of land on which to build a log church. This served for 10 years before a larger building was erected.

It was stated that one of the first cares of this pious colony was to build a house of the Lord. "They were content to dwell themselves in shanties not more comfortable than potato cellars, while their labours were most especially given to the erection of a house of worship, and a manse or parsonage for their minister, according to the custom in their native land".

The Williamsburg church was organised according to the constitution and discipline of the then Church of Scotland. Rules were tight: sinners stood trial and were censured, and the Sabbath was strictly kept. In Calvinistic tradition, the church was the religious, judicial and social centre of the Williamsburg community.

However, historical records show that a few people in frontier settlements like Williamsburg did not always adhere to the high standards of the Presbyterian faith and on occasions they needed a sharp rebuke from church elders.

The "pernicious" practices which earned a rebuke were dancing, horse racing and treating at funerals. "Drinking at the burial of the dead prevailed to a melancholy degree" - Howe's History of the American Presbyterian Church relates.

Schisms developed in the Williamsburg church when a fresh influx of Scots-Irish settlers arrived in the region about 1770. These people, according to Zion Church records, were more liberal in their theological views than the earlier settlers. In 1782, the Rev. Samuel Kennedy arrived from Ireland to occupy the Williamsburg pulpit and his liberal doctrines, which, it is claimed, included the "denial" of the Divinity of Christ, caused major upheaval in the five years of his ministry there.

The liberal faction soon outnumbered the conservatives and the minority withdrew to establish a separate congregation, known as Bethel. The bitterness increased to the point where the minority grouping, on an August night in 1786, razed the old church to the ground. The majority obtained successful legal redress for the action and this led to an irrevocable split.

The friction continued over the next two decades, until March, 1805, when four families from the conservative grouping - the Armstrongs, Blakeleys, Friersons and Fultons - set their sights on lush new lands in the Franklin / Columbia region of middle Tennessee.

Within a year, 10 additional families - the Dickeys, Flemings, Witherspoons, Stephensons and more Friersons - made the 600-mile trek westwards in covered wagons, to be joined in 1808 by Revolutionary War veteran the Rev. James White Stephenson (a pastor at Bethel), Dr. Samuel Mayes, Robert Frierson and James Frierson and their families.

They settled in an area of eight square miles (5,000 acres of lush highly productive land) purchased from the heirs of General Nathanial Greene, a part of the 25,000 acres in Maury County granted to him for services in the Revolutionary War. The purchase price was 15,360 dollars.

At the time there were only a few inhabitants in Maury County, with no settlement older than three years. The region was not inhabited by the Red Indians. They used it as hunting grounds, moving in from other parts of Tennessee. Zion Church was set up and the sacrament of the Lord's Supper was celebrated for for the first time there in August, 1809 with 54 communicants.

The Rev. James White Stephenson was a benevolent man and is credited by being the first pastor in the region to evangelise the black slaves. Many of the settlers in Williamsburg and Maury had slaves and not long after Zion church was formed blacks were admitted into full congregational membership. The Church gallery was reserved to seat the blacks, who, by the mid-19th century, were beginning to outnumber the whites in the congregation.

After the Civil War, the picture changed and sadly the former slaves moved away from Zion to form the Salem Church nearby. Only one remained, Uncle Andy, who stayed to pump the old hand organ at Sunday services.

One legacy of the black community in Zion today is the slave cemetery which lies in the church grounds, not far from where the other worshippers are buried. In Zion, the church elders afforded the slaves the dignity of their own cemetery, although most of the graves are unidentified.

The middle Tennessee settlement of these conservative Presbyterian descendants of the early Drumbo and Knockbracken immigrants prospered and, through the 19th and 20th centuries, members figured prominently in the development of the political, economic, cultural and social life of the region. They were a people who believed that the Bible was the complete and written word of God; they believed in the Trinity and their descendants still hold to the fundamentals of the Reformed faith.

Today, Zion Church is a landmark in middle-Tennessee - a spot where the tenets of Presbyterianism are observed conservatively, but sincerely by a congregation patently aware of the sacrifices of humble descendants from Co. Down who left the nearby port of Belfast in wooden sailing ships to secure a religious freedom that was denied them in their homeland by the Episcopal powers of the day.

Drumbo is a townland which lies halfway between the city of Belfast and Lisburn, the second largest borough (to Belfast) in Northern Ireland. Although so close to larger city life it is still largely an area of farmland. Nearby Knockbracken is more of a suburb of Belfast, largely developed with urban dwellers and now part of the borough of Castlereagh.

15

Rogersville: *frontier town with roots in Ulster*

The small town of Rogersville in Upper East Tennessee was founded by a Cookstown (Co. Tyrone) man and its only hotel was set up by a Coleraine-born Co. Londonderry lawyer who was also a pioneer in the region close on 200 years ago. Frontiersman Davy Crockett whose forebears came from the Castlederg area of Co. Tyrone has also strong connections with Rogersville (population 5,000).

Rogersville was originally known as Carter's Valley, named after the first white settler in the region Colonel John Carter of Virginia. Tyrone-born Joseph Rogers was one of the Ulster-Scots settlers who came down the Shenandoah Valley in Virginia in the late 18th century and moved into Tennessee, just as the frontier lands were being opened up. He arrived at a spot at the Holston River known as Crockett's Creek and was so taken by the beauty of the scenic rolling hills and lush valley that he decided to go no further.

Rogersville was set up in 1786 right on the path of the Avery Trace, a rambling narrow trail to Fort Nashborough (Nashville). On this route in 1801 the Natchez Trace was opened between Nashville and Mississippi. Though Rogersville was initially a log cabin settlement, by 1810 fine brick buildings began to appear.

The elopement in 1786 of Joseph Rogers and Mary Amis, daughter of a prominent man in the North Carolina legislature Captain Thomas Amis, is a favourite Tennessean love story and today the pair lie side by side in a quiet cemetery in Rogersville.

The 1770 Treaty of Lochaber, conducted over colonial North Carolina and the Cherokee lands, granted permission for white settlements in Indian territory. Today, these form the North Eastern Tennessee towns of Rogersville, Elizabethton, Jonesboro and Kingsport.

After the Revolutionary War, the frontier lands were opened up to bounty land settlers. These were veterans of the Revolution who were entitled to land grants. Often they received 1,000 acres or more, depending on their rank and on the service they rendered in the War.

In 1780, Thomas Amis obtained a land grant of 1,000 acres on Big Creek near present-day Rogersville. Settlement in the Rogersville area was rapid. Down the Valley of Virginia came the young sons of old Virginian aristocracy, together with the Scots-Irish and English immigrant frontiersmen and adventurers.

The red-headed Joseph Rogers had been involved as a miller, tanner, blacksmith and distiller in the area and today buried alongside him in the Rogers' cemetery are the grandparents of Davy Crockett, who were massacred by the Indians in the area in 1777.

The Crocketts had been putting in their crops in the fields and were attacked before they could return to the safety of their cabin. They had a son who was taken away by the Indians and kept for about 20 years. Up until the beginning of the 19th century, Indians roamed this part of East Tennessee and their violent run-ins with the tough Scots-Irish settlers are part of the folklore here.

The legendary Davy himself was born in a neighbouring county - not on a mountain top, as the movie moguls would try to convince us, but in a hollow at the mouth of the Limestone River. His people, originally French Huguenot Protestants, were Scots-Irish Presbyterians who moved from the North Tyrone / East Donegal area to America during the early 18th century. Crockett, who was killed at the Alamo, was, as well as being a fearless Indian and Mexican fighter and bear hunter, a leading Tennessee politician.

Hugh Campbell, another Scots-Irish settler, is also buried in the same cemetery as Joseph Rogers and the Crocketts. He was a Rogersville merchant and close friend of Joseph Rogers. A letter written by Campbell to Rogers on June 28, 1801 (with a Philadelphia postmark) tells how a ship had arrived at New Castle, Delaware from Derry with "700 brave Irish men from Derry" and he hoped to see them before returning back to Rogersville.

John Augustine McKinney is another Ulsterman who figured prominently in the landscape of Rogersville in its early formative years and
today the Hale Springs Inn along Main Street is testimony of his influence there. He was a large ebullient and outgoing man (six feet-plus in
height), well mannered and always dressed like a gentleman. He quickly
rose to prominence as an attorney in Tennessee and was considered the
top legal man on the frontier of the day.

McKinney, the youngest of five brothers, left Coleraine, then listed
as a part of Co. Antrim, as a 19-year-old in 1800 to seek fame and
fortune in America. His fine education in Ireland, and at Edinburgh
University, and the taking of a medicine degree after landing in the
States, ensured he was a young man of standing by the time he reached
the frontier lands.

He began a law practice in 1807 in the Knoxville area and became a
contemporary of arguably the most illustrious Tennessean Andrew
Jackson, who was born within two years of his parents leaving
Carrickfergus and who went on to serve two terms as United States
President.

McKinney, who also became an extensive land owner, rose to the
position of US District Attorney when John Quincy Adams was President in the 1820s and was chosen as a representative to the Tennessee
state constitutional convention in 1832-34. A nephew Robert J.
McKinney, also born in Coleraine, was one of Tennessee's foremost
judges in the mid-19th century.

A 'History of Tennessee' records this tribute: "John A. McKinney's
great success was due to his thorough knowledge of the law, his untiring
perserverance and his incorruptible (sic) integrity".

John Augustine McKinney was said to be a man who was interested
in building up the religious, educational and material welfare of the
country. This obviously came from his strict Presbyterian Church up-
bringing - he was a ruling elder in the First Presbyterian Church set up
in Rogersville in 1805 - and his home was open-house for ministers,
teachers and others who found there a hearty welcome, a generous sympathiser and a delightful resting place.

Although a black slave owner himself, as many men of his position
in the Tennessee of the early 19th century were, John A. McKinney
considered slavery to be "an evil we must be rid of as soon as
possible."

"We can't get rid of it overnight, but we must do it as soon as possible or there will be a real calamity", said McKinney, who saw the solution to slavery a form of share cropping. He did not live long enough to see the practice abolished, but in his will he decreed that he did not want to see the slave families on his estate broken up.

It was in 1806 that John A. McKinney first came to Rogersville, for a law hearing representing a client from Philadelphia. He was so impressed by the area that he decided to remain and by 1810 had built a beautiful white brick mansion there with green shutters and tall chimneys, along the lines of the big houses he had known in his native Ulster homeland.

The house, at McKinney Avenue / Colonial Road facing Crockett Creek and beside an oak tree 500 years old, is still standing and inhabited. He lived there with his wife Eliza and seven children. Before he settled in Rogersville, McKinney had been in correspondence with Joseph Rogers and, in one letter (postmarked Philadelphia January 16, 1805), he talked of a most severe winter where some of the poorer settlers had perished from cold and hunger.

Rogersville became an important legal centre for the East Tennessee region and was highly influential in the politics of the state. Nearly everyone who was anyone in Tennessee at the time visited Rogersville regularly, including Andrew Jackson and two other Tennesseans of Ulster-Scots roots with Presidential ambitions - James K. Polk and Andrew Johnson, and John A. McKinney felt that the town needed an elegant dwelling house for its important visitors.

In 1824, he ordered the building of a large three-storey building, to be known as the McKinney Tavern House. It was run by members of McKinney's family and rapidly became a main stopping-off point for the stage coach trade of the day. Andrew Jackson, 'Old Hickory' to many admirers in Tennessee, visited the Tavern House many times - the last in 1832 after his first term as President.

John A. McKinney, described as the best friend Upper East Tennessee and Rogersville ever had, died suddenly in 1845, aged 64. His Coleraine-born four brothers and sister all came to America and also made their mark.

The eldest brother the Rev. James McKinney was an eminent minister of the Reformed Presbyterian Church in America, having graduated from Glasgow University in 1778 in medicine and theology. Two brothers were doctors - Samuel practised in Philadelphia and Rogersville and Archibald in Philadelphia and Cincinnati. Robert McKinney settled in Pittsburg and sister Sarah lived at Chester in South Carolina.

By 1867 the Tavern had passed out of family hands, sold to Samuel Neill, another of Scots-Irish roots, for 4,000 dollars. Sammy Neill, as he was known to his Rogersville townsfolk, was quite a character and in his later years he would sit on the porch of the Tavern, greeting people as they passed by on the migrant trail to Kentucky through the Cumberland Gap.

"Where are you going to strangers?", he would call out. "We are on our way to 'Kaintuck' if the good Lord will show us the way", was the reply. Their wagons were clean and painted and their covers were clean. Many returned through Rogersville with the wagons torn and muddy and old Sammy Neill would call out: "Oh stranger, where are you heading?"   "Back where we came from if the good Lord gives us the strength".   Back to Tennessee and Virginia, for Kentucky was still a wild, fearsome and inhospitable place in those days.

During the American Civil War of 1861-65 the McKinney Tavern House was used as the headquarters and hospital for the Confederate Army. By 1884, it was renamed Hale Springs Inn in keeping with the increasing popularity of mineral springs in the area and it had several owners before it was taken over in the early 1980s by Captain Carl Netherland-Brown, a descendant of John A. McKinney and John Netherland, another important political figure in Tennessee.

Captain Netherland-Brown, a retired sea captain who was in charge of the US vessel SS Bahama Star, remains the Inn's owner and he exudes great pride at the accomplishments of the Ulster-Scots who were the first settlers in the region.

The Kyles are another Scots-Irish family with strong ties and achievement in the Rogersville area. They can trace their roots back to Ayrshire and Co. Tyrone (Mournebeg and Brackey) and Co. Londonderry (Dungiven). Brothers Robert and David Kyle left Co. Tyrone about 1740 and settled in Virginia. Robert's son Robert made it to East Tennessee and as a captain in the Revolutionary War, he commanded a garrison of soldiers against the Indians at Hawkins County in 1777, the year the Crocketts were massacred.

In 1785, he established a home at Walnut Hill, seven miles west of present-day Rogersville. He had seven children, one of whom Jane was scalped by the Indians at her front gate. She recovered with only the loss of her hair.

Absalom Kyle, a son of Robert Jun., married into an aristocratic family the Cobbs and, though he and his wife Bathsheba started out together in a humble log cabin because her father opposed the marriage, he eventually prospered by establishing the stage coach route between Atlanta and Washington through Rogersville.

In those days, the stage coach travelled 25 miles a day and with Rogersville 240 miles from Nashville and 70 from Knoxville movement between these main centres of population was slow. Bathsheba was only 15 when they were wed for these were the days when an ummarried girl over 18 was generally referred to as "a hopeless old maid".

By 1818, the pair had a large brick home built at Walnut Hill for them and their 14 children, one of whom William Caswell Kyle was a general in the Confederate Army during the Civil War. A brother Leonidas Netherland Kyle was a Confederate Army captain and his son Gale Porter Kyle married Gladys Boone, a direct descendant of Daniel Boone, the English pioneer who set up the Wilderness Road to Kentucky which passed through Rogersville. And there was also James Woods Rogan, of solid Co. Tyrone Presbyterian stock, who was a leading naturalist and public figure in Tennessee during the 19th century.

Rooms in the Hale Springs Inn - a boarding house re-modelled on the style of the early 19th century period - are named after the people who put Rogersville on the map: John Augustine McKinney, Joseph Rogers, James Woods Rogan and John Netherland and the political luminaries who stayed there - Andrew Jackson, James K. Polk and Andrew Johnson.

Except to a few, Rogersville is relatively unheard of in Northern Ireland, but it is a place where Ulsterman and women staked a claim to civilisation and a new and prosperous life in what was almost a barren wilderness 200 years ago.

16

How the Scots-Irish *shaped religion in Tennessee*

Presbyterianism was the first Christian denomination to be established in Tennessee and this was largely due to the influence of the Scots-Irish settlers. The first Presbyterian minister to visit the region was the Rev. Charles Cummings from Abingdon, Virginia and in 1772 he ministered to two congregations which had sprung up on the banks of the Holston River which then was in North Carolina and today is in East Tennessee.

Cummings was in the mould of the frontier settlers he preached to : tough and direct, with a message that was fundamental to the spiritual needs of those who inhabited this wild and desolate country. Travelling on horseback, Cummings carried a long rifle as a precaution and every man in his congregation also had a gun at his side, just in case of a sudden Indian attack.

In 1775 another Presbyterian minister the Rev. Joseph Rhea preached at the Holston settlement. He had moved from a congregation in Co. Donegal, Ireland in 1769 and erected a church in Maryland. During his short spell on the Holston he bought a plot of land, but when he returned to get his family in Maryland he died.

The trail Cummings and Rhea took was followed within a few years by yet another preacher of Ulster-Scots vintage the Rev. Samuel Doak and in 1777 he became the first resident minister in the region we now know of as East Tennessee.

Doak, fired with an evangelistic zeal, was the son of a Co. Antrim small farmer who emigrated with his four brothers and two sisters to

Pennsylvania in 1740 and moved to Virginia to settle in Augusta County. The young Samuel Doak was born there in 1749 and his rise to the ministry was greatly influenced by the Rev. Robert Smith, who had emigrated from Londonderry as a small boy.

Soon after his ordination in 1777 Samuel Doak moved into the East Tennessee region on receiving a call from the Hopewell and Concord congregations in the North Holston River settlement in Sullivan County. For two years he provided what was literally the only religious leadership in this thinly populated wilderness, before moving on to the adjoining Washington County to become pastor of a church at Salem.

Samuel Doak, a most energetic man, was considered to be not only a good pastor, but an aggressive evangelist as well. After forming the church at Salem, he established congregations at New Providence, Carter's Valley, Mount Bethel, Upper Concord, New Bethel and Hebron, all in East Tennessee. It was said of him: "This stern hard God-fearing man became a most powerful influence for good throughout the whole formative period for Tennessee".

Doak not only built churches, he founded schools and pioneered education in the region in a manner befitting his Presbyterian ministerial calling. His two sons John Whitefield and Samuel Witherspoon followed their father into the ministry and they too lit a flame for Christ on the frontier.

A graduate of Samuel Doak's Tusculum Academy was Gideon Blackburn, who with all the fire and energy of his teacher went on to proclaim the Christian message to those who were moving into middle Tennessee. Blackburn not only preached to the white settlers, he brought the scriptures to the Cherokee Indians and enjoyed relative success in conversions among the tribes.

Through the 1790s as Tennessee was in its infancy as a state, Gideon Blackburn led in the establishment of churches in Knoxville and Nashville (then Fort Nashborough). The gospel had been taken across the Cumberland Mountains to the forts and the stations where the people were huddled together for safety in numbers. The seeds of Christianity were being sown.

Other Presbyterian clerics followed in Doak and Blackburn: Hezekiah Balch moved from North Carolina; Samuel Carrick and Isaac Anderson from Virginia. Balch evoked controversy in the region when he accepted a doctrine known as Hopkinsianism, which was a marked departure from the traditional concept of Calvinism and ministerial colleagues distanced themselves from his teaching.

Samuel Carrick founded the congregation at Lebanon in the Fork, about five miles from Knoxville, and after setting up the First Knoxville congregation, he opened a school which was to evolve into Blount College, East Tennessee University and today the University of Tennessee. Isaac Anderson was also a preacher and teacher of some standing in the Tennessee Valley region and he established Maryville College.

In 1796 when Tennessee became a state there were 27 Presbyterian congregations from East Tennessee to the Nashville belt, their existence due in no small measure to the determination of the Scots-Irish people to keep their Calvinistic form of faith alive on the frontier.

Eight years earlier, in 1788, a General Assembly of the United States was formed with four synods. New York and New Jersey, Philadelphia, Virginia and the Carolinas. There were 16 Presbyteries, 177 ministers, 111 probationers and 419 churches.

The Baptists were on the scene in Tennessee soon after the Presbyterians and with a more simpler form of ministerial calling they did not experience much difficulty founding congregations on the frontier.

Tennessee had two main types of Baptists: the Regular Baptists were strict Calvinists who had withdrawn from established New England denominations during the Great Awakening revival prior to the Revolutionary War. By 1787, most Baptists in Tennessee were merged under the term United Baptists, with each congregation having been formed before there were pastors to serve them.

Like the Presbyterians the Baptists moved first into the Holston River region of East Tennessee and branched out across the Cumberland Mountains to middle Tennessee. But unlike Presbyterian ministers, Baptist pastors did not need to be specially ordained at universities and theological colleges. They were largely of the farmer-preacher variety who laboured the land through the week and on Sundays took their place in the pulpit to proclaim the word of the Lord.

Baptist pastors on the frontier were highly colourful individuals, who very often engaged in fire and brimstone type of preaching. Services were conducted with great fervour.

Methodists, the adherents of the preaching of John Wesley, arrived in Tennessee after the Presbyterians and Baptists and the first congregations were formed in the Watauga, Holston and Nolichucky River settlements as the Revolutionary War was ending in the early 1780s. Methodism had fraternal links with the Church of England and this led to prejudice and suspicion from many settlers, particularly the Scots-Irish, that Methodists were too sympathetic to the British position. Eventually Methodism became Americanised and prospered, due to the zeal of ministerial circuit riders equipped with their Bibles, hymn books containing the inspirational verses of Charles Wesley and pamphlets with the sermons of John Wesley.

Most who pioneered the early American frontier in the late 18th century had some basic concept of religion, but only a minority held offical church membership. The residents of the new settlements had concentrated on the material need to survive amd many showed a marked indifference to religion. It took several decades of aggressive witnessing by the Presbyterians, the Baptists and the Methodists for church life to be firmly established in the mainstream and it was through revivalist meetings that religion took a solid grip on Tennessean society. Today Tennessee is one of the most church orientated states in America, with Protestant fundamentalism a dominant strain.

During the early part of the 19th century other denominations took root in Tennessee, among them the Episcopal Church and the Roman Catholic Church. Episcopalians were linked to the Anglican community (the Church of England) and the ramifications of the Revolutionary War delayed their church from establishing in Tennessee. It was not until the 1820s that a congregation could be formed, in Franklin.

In the period leading to the settlement of Tennessee Roman Catholics were few in number in the state, with no resident priests and no established churches. By the early 19th century priests were travelling in from Kentucky to conduct masses to the scattered faithful, but it was not until 1830 that the first parish was formed in the state, in Nashville. Membership increased significantly by the mid-19th century when Irish workers arrived with the building of the railways and new parishes sprung up to the west and to the east. The Roman Catholic religion, however, in Tennessee could never rival the numbers and influence of the main Protestant denominations.

East Tennessee had a small number of Jewish settlers in the late 18th century, but Judaism did not become properly organised in the state until 1851 and today the sect would not have a large membership there when compared with that of other American states, particularly on the eastern seaboard.

Today in Tennessee the Baptist churches have by far the largest number of members, Methodists are the second largest denomination and Pentecostalists (Church of God and Elim) are now much more numerous than Presbyterians of different strands. The Roman Catholic, Episcopal and Jewish denominations are much smaller in number.

There are various strands of Presbyterianism in America - the mainstream Church of the USA has almost four million adherants and the smaller groupings like Reformed, Orthodox, Evangelical and Cumberland Presbyterian number about 400,000 members.

Cumberland Presbyterians are peculiar to Tennessee, Kentucky, and the adjoining Carolina states and the denomination's origins date back to the Scots-Irish settlement of the late 18th century.

After the Revolutionary War there was a brief period of "spiritual lethargy" in the new nation. However, the revival, known as the second Great Awakening (the first Great Awakening came from the preaching of George Whitefield in the mid-18th century) led to religious expansion for denominations like the Presbyterians. In order to meet the challenge, the Presbyterians and the Congregational churches in 1801 entered into an offical policy of co-operation which was known as the Plan of Union.

Tens of thousands of people were moving away from the established settlements along the Atlantic seaboard to the West: Tennessee, Virginia, Kentucky, The Carolinas, Ohio, and Indinia. Neither denomination by itself had a sufficient number of ministers to keep up with the influx into the new settlements, so they joined hands. But the explosion was so great in Tennessee and Kentucky that even the united efforts of Congregationalists and Presbyterians were insufficient to keep up with the pastoral work demand.

For Presbyterians there was only one source in the United States for a trained ministry - Princeton - and there were simply not enough graduates to meet the need. The Baptists and Methodists, having a more flexible organisation and lower requiremants for ordination, seized the initiative Some Presbyterians wanted to lower the standards for qualification for the ministry and also to loosen the connection between American Presbyterians and the Calvinism of the Westminster Standards, which they felt was "not as compatible" with revivalism as a more

Armenian theology would have been. This resulted in a very bitter debate, with the result that some Presbyterians withdrew and formed the Cumberland Presbyterian Church in 1810.

The Cumberland church adopted the position that "spiritually-minded men" who felt the call to the ministry and had preaching gifts should be ordained whether or not they had a "proper" theological education. They also removed from their doctrinal standards what they saw as the offensive sections, primarily on the doctrines of double predestination and human will, while still adhering to the Westminister Standards in all the other parts.

Because the centre of this controversy was in the area of the Cumberland River, they took the name of the Cumberland Presbyterian Church and the original meeting of this new denomination was held a few miles west of Nashville. In 1906 the Presbyterian Church USA and the Cumberland Presbyterians voted to reunite, but about a third of the Cumberland membership did not join and today their numbers are around 100,000, concentrated in the rural areas of Tennessee, Kentucky, and the Carolinas.

• Figures from the official church membership survey in Tennessee in 1990 show Baptists (of various strands) 1,654,533; Methodists 419,506; Church of Christ 219,996; Roman Catholics 137,203; Presbyterians (of various strands) 132,344; Church of God 64,731; Episcopals 40,351; Assembly of God 31,630; Seventh Day Adventists 27,119; Church of the Nazarene 23,392; Lutherans 13,981; Jews 17,461, Latter Day Saints 15,635. The church membership in Tennessee of 2,964,916 represents 61.2 per cent of the total population. There are an estimated 10,000 churches in the state.

SAMUEL DOAK: PIONEERING PASTOR ON THE FRONTIER

No American frontier pastor earned the acclaim of his people quite like the Rev. Samuel Doak, the son of a Co. Antrim man who moved to the valley of Virginia with other members of his family.

The severe winter of 1739-40 in the north of Ireland - it became known as "the time of the black frost" - drove thousands of Ulster Presbyterians to emigrate to the new lands across the Atlantic. Among them were the five Doak brothers (John, Nathaniel, Robert, David and Samuel) and two sisters (Ann and Thankful). On the journey across Samuel Doak married one of his kith Jane Mitchell, a widow with three daughters. They moved through Pennsylvania to Virginia in the great trek of the Scots-Irish and settled upon lands at Augusta County.

The Rev. Samuel Doak was born in Virginia nine years after his parents' arrival and he grew up in the most hazardous frontier existence, working on the family farm until he was 16, always with an eye open for Indian attack.

The Doaks were a God-fearing people, who, while they were far removed from their established churches, adhered rigidly to the teachings of the Bible, catechisms and the Presbyterian Confession of Faith they had brought with them from Co. Antrim. Samuel Doak was greatly influenced by the piety of his parents and as a teenager he made his "profession of religion" and began studies for the ministry, both in Virginia and in Maryland.

As a student Doak fell under the influence of the Rev. Robert Smith, who had emigrated from Londonderry as a young boy, and for a while he taught at Smith's school in Pequea, Pennsylvania.

Soon after being ordained as a minister in 1777 Samuel Doak did missionary work in south west Virginia, but it was a call from the Hopewell and Concord congregations in the North Holston River settlement in Sullivan County, North Carolina (now East Tennessee) which settled his destiny. Samuel Doak was the first resident Presbyterian minister to witness in Tennessee and about 1778 he established the first church and first schoolhouse in the new world west of the Alleghenics.

President Theodore Roosevelt, in 'The Winning of the West', wrote of Doak: "Possessed of the vigorous energy that marks the true pioneer spirit, he determined to cast in his lot with the frontier folk. He walked through Maryland and Virginia, driving before him an old 'flea-bitten grey' horse, loaded with a sackful of books; crossed the Alleghenies, and came down along the blazed trails to the Holston settlements. The hardy people among whom he took up his abode were to appreciate his learning and religion as much as they admired his adventurous and indomitable temper; and the stern, hard, God-fearing man became a most powerful influence for good throughout the whole formative period of the South West".

The settlement Samuel Doak joined was of pioneering stock like himself and the two factors which united them was their faith, and survival from the harshness of the environment; hostile native Indian tribes and the advances of the British colonial forces.

Doak was by then married and it is related that on one occasion while he was absent from home obtaining provisions his wife Esther and baby miraculously escaped a Cherokee Indian attack. The barking of dogs alerted Esther Doak to the approach of Indians and with the baby asleep in her arms she slipped quietly into the woods. From her hiding place she anxiously watched the Indians enter the log cabin, carry out some of the furniture and set fire to the building.

Remarkably the baby did not wake; for if it had and started to cry she and the child would have faced almost certain death from the Cherokees. When the Indians departed she went after dark, by a blind path, to the nearest frontier station, where she met up with her husband the next day.

Samuel Doak ministered for two years in Sullivan County at the Fork of Watauga and Holston Rivers. He moved to Washington County at the Little Limestone River in South Holston, near the spot where legendary frontiersman Davy Crockett was born and grew up.

The threat of Indian attack was with the settlers daily, and, more than once, Samuel Doak's sermon was interrupted by a messenger bringing news of Cherokee savagery. On each occasion Doak would automatically pray to God for deliverance and abandon his meeting to join the other men in pursuit of the enemy. Doak's rifle was always at his side during services. Samuel Doak not only preached; he was the main teacher in the settlement and he founded not only dozens of churches in East Tennessee but schools as well.

A momentous hour for Samuel Doak came at Sycamore Shoals at Elizabethton in East Tennessee on September 25, 1780. There the Overmountain Men were mustering before the Battle of Kings Mountain and Colonel John Sevier asked the much respected pastor to speak to them.

A vital stage had been reached in the Revolutionary War and the Wataugans, composed mainly of Scots-Irish families, were determined to breach the order of King George III of England that they were not to make further inroads on to the lands held by the Indians, west of the Allegheny Mountains.

The King's top soldier, Aberdonian Colonel Patrick Ferguson headed an army of Redcoats ready to crush the settlers, but there was a shock in store for them from the revolutionaries led by four redoubtable men: Ulster-Scots Colonel Charles McDowell and Colonel William Campbell; Welshman Colonel Isaac Shelby and French Huguenot Colonel John Sevier.

On the morning of September 25 the men gathered with their families at Sycamore Shoals for a religious service, conducted by the Rev. Samuel Doak. The fiery sermon and prayer that Doak delivered that day steeled the Overmountain Men for the march up Gap Creek to the impending confrontation with the Redcoats, echoing the Old Testament battle cry - "The Sword of the Lord and Gideon".

Doak's words may have been characteristic of a cleric in the turbulent years of the late 18th century, but in the years since, they have struck a chord with millions of Americans who strongly cherish the liberty secured by the events at Kings Mountain.

SAMUEL DOAK'S SERMON AND PRAYER AT SYCAMORE SHOALS MUSTER SEPTEMBER 25, 1780

"My countrymen, you are about to set out on an expedition which is full of hardships and dangers, but one in which the Almighty will attend you. The Mother Country has her hands upon you, these American colonies, and takes that for which our fathers planted their homes in the wilderness - OUR LIBERTY.

"Taxation without representation and the quartering of soldiers in the homes of our people without their consent are evidence that the Crown of England would take from its American subjects the last vestige of freedom. Your brethren across the mountains are crying like Macedonia unto your help. God forbid that you shall refuse to hear and answer their call - but the call of your brethren is not all. The enemy is marching hither to destroy your homes.

"Brave men, you are not unacquainted with battle. Your hands have already been taught to war and your fingers to fight. You have wrested these beautiful valleys of the Holston and Watauga from the savage hand. Will you tarry now until the other enemy carries fire and sword to your very doors? No, it shall not be. Go forth then in the strength of your manhood to the aid of your brethren, the defence of your liberty and the protection of your homes. And may the God of justice be with you and give you victory.

"Let Us Pray.

"Almighty and gracious God! Thou hast been the refuge and strength of Thy people in all ages. In time of sorest need we have learned to come to Thee - our Rock and our Fortress. Thou knowest the dangers and snares that surround us on march and in battle. Thou knowest the dangers that constantly threaten the humble, but well beloved homes, which Thy servants have left behind them.

"O, in Thine infinite mercy, save us from the cruel hand of the savage, and of tyrant. Save the unprotected homes while fathers and husbands and sons are far away fighting for freedom and helping the oppressed. Thou, who promised to protect the sparrow in its flight, keep ceaseless watch, by day and by night, over our loved ones. The helpless woman and little children, we commit to Thy care. Thou wilt not leave them or forsake them in times of loneliness and anxiety and terror.

"O, God of Battle, arise in Thy might. Avenge the slaughter of Thy people. Confound those who plot for our destruction. Crown this mighty effort with victory, and smite those who exalt themselves against liberty and justice and truth. Help us as good soldiers to wield the SWORD OF THE LORD AND GIDEON".

"AMEN".

The British forces were routed by the Overmountain militia, Colonel Patrick Ferguson was killed and 225 of his men lay dead after a battle which lasted 65 minutes. For the victors their loss was small - 28 dead and 62 wounded, with the capture of 800 Redcoats and as much booty as they could lay their hands on. Kings Mountain was the turning point in the Revolutionary War and for the Scots-Irish militia men it was the sign to ignore the King and move on to new frontiers.

Samuel Doak, meanwhile, removed himself to the battlefield he knew best, winning souls for Christ and he was instrumental in opening new churches in other parts of East Tennessee, including Carter's Valley where Ulster-born settlers like Joseph Rogers and the Crocketts had set up home.

By 1785, Doak had organised Abingdon Presbytery under the axis of the Synod of Philadelphia and incorporating the churches of East Tennessee and south west Virginia. Within a decade this Presbytery extended to 36 congregations and a dozen ministers. Doak founded the Martin Academy and until the beginning of the 19th century it was the main seat of learning in this most westerly part of the frontier. It became Washington College in 1795.

The austere Calvinism Doak stood for left its mark on the community he served and it was said "his habits were those of the student, teacher and divine". One of the first graduates of Washington College was Doak's son John Whitefield, who with his brother Samuel Witherspoon became Presbyterian ministers.

The Doaks had six children, two sons and four daughters in their marriage of 30 - odd years, which ended with Esther Doak's death in 1807. In 1818, the same year that he resigned as president of Washington College, Samuel Doak married Margaret McEwen, a widow from Blount County.

On retirement from Washington College, at the age of 69, Doak moved to nearby Greeneville to help his son Samuel Witherspoon with teaching duties at a classical school named Tusculum. He spent the last 12 years of his life there giving "a good and practical education" to up to 70 pupils.

For all his conservatism on theological matters, Samuel Doak was very strongly opposed to slavery, then actively pursued over a large part of the south west territory. His pulpit denunciation led to bitter conflict with some of the leading slave owners in the region and, after personally freeing many blacks, he managed to send them to Ohio to live. The seeds of his anti-slavery principles were implanted in the minds of many of his students and this influence significantly harnessed the move towards the abolition of slavery some years after his death.

Doak's death on December 12, 1830 brought the frontier faithful to a standstill and when his remains were buried in Salem Presbyterian churchyard a multitude from a wide area gathered to pay their last respects. This man of learning and religion probably did more for Christianity on the American frontier than any other living soul.

He was "the first apostle of Presbyterianism in Tennessee" ..... "the pioneer of education in Tennessee" - the missionary stalwart who "educated and sent into Tennessee and the adjoining states a very large proportion of the church ministry and other professions who moulded the character of the early population and founded their civil and religious institutions".

Samuel Doak, in the best Calvinist tradition, led his people through a wilderness and pointed them in the right direction, both spiritually and educationally. The light that he shone on the frontier was an inspiration to so many and not surprisingly his memory lives on.

HOLY GROUND AT LEBANON IN THE FORK

One of the most beautiful acres in Tennessee if not in the entire United States is the site of the first church in the Knoxville valley region. It was there that Presbyterian minister the Rev. Samuel Carrick came to minister to the first wave of Scots-Irish settlers who had set up home on the fertile banks of the Holston and French Broad Rivers, now the Tennessee River which flows through Knoxville city.

Lebanon in the Fork could not have been a more appropriate and serene setting for the worship of God in what was then a virtual wilderness. Surrounded by 11 tall cedar trees and in full view of the idyllic fork which linked the winding Holston and French Broad Rivers, the Rev. Carrick used as his pulpit an old Indian mound for the first open-air service. And the text that he chose for his sermon that day was Second Corinthians chapter 5, verse 20 - "Now then, we are ambassadors for Christ as though God did beseech you by us; we pray you in God's stead, by ye reconciled to God".

Samuel Carrick, like the people he was ministering to at Lebanon in the Fork, was Scots-Irish. His parents were born in Ulster and had moved about the mid-18th century to York County, Virginia, where Samuel was born.

Soon after his licensure as a minister in 1782, Samuel Carrick was moved by the urgent need to take the message of the gospel to the frontier lands of the south west and it was while searching for people he had known back in Virginia that he wandered on a group of hunters and trappers living by the fork at the Holston / French Broad Rivers.

These settlers - they included James White, Robert Love, James Connor, George McNutt and Francis Ramsey, all veterans of the Revolutionary War - were eking out a rough, tough existence from log cabin homes and risking their lives in a region heavily populated by Cherokee Indians.

Coming upon the frontiersmen, Samuel Carrick explained that he was a Presbyterian minister and wished to establish a church. The men urged him to stay, which he did, and after sending word to the group for which he was searching, they made an appointment for him to preach several Sundays later.

It was 1791 and folk from miles away, hungry to hear the word of God, gathered around the simple Indian mound pulpit for the first organised service in that part of Tennessee. Their curiousity after the old religion had brought them to their knees.

While Mr. Carrick was preaching, another minister the Rev. Hezekiah Balch appeared and was invited to speak. Convinced that the text from Second Corinthians had not been exhausted, Mr. Balch continued to develop it without repeating the thoughts expressed by Samuel Carrick. Lebanon in the Fork had become hallowed ground.

Preaching, camp meeting style, continued for several days and some parents had their children baptised. The services led to the formation of the Church called Lebanon in the Fork and Samuel Carrick stayed on as the minister.

James White, along with George McNutt, was a founding elder at the Church, but within a year further explorations brought White five miles up stream to First Creek (now down-town Knoxville). By late 1792, he had given over his turnip patch for the erection of the First Presbyterian Church in Knoxville. White was said to be a man with a fondness for turnips.

Lebanon in the Fork prospered as a congregation, taking in many of the families who had come to settle at the Holston / French Broad fork. The original church building was constructed of unhewn logs and modestly extended only 20 feet square. By 1793, the congregation had increased so much that a larger structure had to be erected, reaching out 40 by 60 feet with well-hewn logs and having a well-ordered interior.

For a long period the new Church was the most imposing meeting house in the region and the original building was converted into a session hall. A cemetery was developed and among the first burials was that of Samuel Carrick's wife Elizabeth Moore.

Her funeral, in September, 1793, took place on the day of a threatened attack by Indians on James White's Fort Knox and all the male settlers, including the Rev. Samuel Carrick, were called upon to bear arms in defence. This left only the women of the Lebanon in the Fork congregation to take the remains of Mrs. Carrick down the Holston River in a canoe, for burial at the cemetery. Such were the pressing dangers of the day that Samuel Carrick could not be present at his wife's funeral.

Samuel Carrick was not only a preacher. He was also much sought after for medical advice and tendered regularly to the sick of his congregation. John Adair, the North Carolina land entry taker who financed the Revolutionary forces for the Battle of Kings Mountain from the state tariffs he lifted, was an elder at Lebanon in the Fork. He later joined James White and George McNutt as a founding elder of First Knoxville Church.

Other notables of the Scots-Irish settlers who were involved in the early years of the congregation were James Armstrong and Robert Houston, who had moved with their families from South Carolina. There was also Frances Alexander Ramsey, an explorer who first visited the area in 1783 to purchase 500 acres of land at the French Broad / Holston River fork. He returned in 1792 to take up residence there and became closely identified with the Rev. Samuel Carrick in his work. A son, Dr. James G. M. Ramsey was a noted historian and wrote the "Annals of Tennessee to the end of the 18th century". Both he and his father are buried in the cemetery at Lebanon in the Fork.

Samuel Carrick, dignified yet forthright in the pulpit, had evangelised a wilderness, bringing his people back to a God they had known in their youth, but had neglected through years traversing the wild frontier. The witness he proclaimed at Lebanon in the Fork swept the Knoxville region like a raging flame and a succession of Presbyterian churches were planted as more settlers moved in, and more clerics of Carrick's stamp followed the frontier trail.

Samuel Carrick became the founding pastor of First Knoxville Church and for a period he looked after the two congregations, as well as holding the presidency of Blount College, which was to be forerunner of the University of Tennessee.

When Knoxville became the capital of the new state of Tennessee in 1796, the settlement had only 40 houses and a population of 400 people. But within a decade the population had grown to several thousand and the congregation of First Knoxville expanded quite rapidly, even though it was 1816 before there was a proper meeting house.

Regrettably, the beloved pastor who had sown the seeds of Christianity in the region took a seizure one Sunday morning in August, 1809, as he prepared for a communion service, and died. Today a plaque stands in the cemetery of First Knoxville honouring its Scots-Irish founding fathers: minister, the Rev. Samuel Carrick and elders James White, John Adair and George McNutt.

First Knoxville is now one of the leading churches in East Tennessee, aligned to the Presbyterian Church (USA) and with a congregation representing a wide diversity of life in Knoxville. There are close on 40 Presbyterian churches in the Knoxville area, scores of Baptist churches of various strands, about two dozen Methodist churches, six Roman Catholic chapels and hundreds of small Protestant fundamentalist groupings.

Knoxville is in the heart of the American "Bible Belt" and it is not only dominated by church spires. The giant sprawl of the Baptist hospital beside the mighty Tennessee River is evidence that this city thrives on its deep religious undercurrent.

Sadly, Lebanon in the Fork - five miles east of the city - is no longer a meeting place for worshippers. The Church was destroyed in a fire on the night of August 25, 1981 and was never rebuilt by a congregation which had dwindled considerably from its peak years of the 19th century. The tombstone of members of the earliest congregations remain, including the final resting place of Elizabeth Moore Carrick.

Standing beneath the cedar trees and alongside the four pillared plinth which marks the spot of the original Lebanon in the Fork Church, as the author did last year, one is struck immediately by the awesome reverence of the place. The beauty of the encircling countryside sets it out as a spot close to heaven.

This was once a church in the wildwood, a sanctified acre where God's faithful servant Samuel Carrick brought the gospel to a people searching for a new destiny in a wilderness of the frontier but desperately eager to reclaim the Presbyterian faith of their fathers.

CHURCH IN THE WILDWOOD

Washington Presbyterian Church, located 10 miles north east of Knoxville, was founded in the summer of 1802 by Scots-Irish settlers who had moved into Knox County from Virginia, North Carolina and Kentucky. They settled in what was then known as "Grassy Valley" and the Rev. Samuel Carrick helped them set up the congregation.

The first minister was the Rev. Isaac Anderson, grandson of Isaac Anderson who was born in Co. Down in 1730 and who arrived in Knox County in 1801 with his son William, from Rockbridge County, Virginia.

William Anderson had five sons - the Rev. Isaac; Robert, a judge; Samuel and William, both lawyers and James, a colonel in the militia. Rev. Isaac Anderson founded Maryville College. The Andersons were the descendants of Samuel Shannon, who fought at the Siege of Londonderry in 1688-89 on behalf of the Williamite forces and moved to America early in the 18th century. His daughter, Mary, married James McCampbell in Virginia and the McCampbells moved with the Andersons and Smiths to Grassy Valley. The families were to become interwoven by marriage.

Washington, named after General George Washington, became the church of many Knoxville valley settlers and even though another congregation was formed nearby at Spring Place in 1842, it continued to prosper.

Later in 1886 in the same area the Shannondale Presbyterian Church came into existence and today all three congregations still co-exist.

The Calvinistic fervour in this area was complemented by an influx of French-Swiss Brethren and Huguenot Protestants in the mid-19th century and some of these families joined the Washington, Spring Place and Shannondale congregations.

THE RHEAS OF DONEGAL AND LONDONDERRY

Few Scots-Irish families can match the illustrious contribution towards the opening up of the American frontier made by the Rheas, starting from the Rev. Joseph Rhea who arrived in Philadelphia from Donegal in Ireland in 1769. The Rheas were descended from the Campbell clan in lowland Scotland and the family line was started by a Matthew Campbell who moved to Fahan in East Donegal around 1665 after being involved in an abortive rebellion against the government of King Charles II.

On arrival in Ulster Campbell changed his name to Rhea (pronounced Ray) and it is known that two of his sons settled in Belfast and another at Kennecalley near St. Johnston in East Donegal. Matthew Campbell Rhea took a prominant part in the Siege of Londonderry in 1688-89 when the Roman Catholic forces of James II laid siege on the Protestant residents of the city.

The Rheas were a strong Presbyterian family and Joseph, a grandson of Matthew, rose to the ministry, graduating at the age of 27 with an MA degree at the University of Glasgow in 1742 and being ordained by the Presbytery of Londonderry. He first preached at the little church at Barracranaugh or Bun Cranaugh (now Buncrana) near the shores of Lough Foyle and for 20 years from 1749 to 1769 was the faithful pastor of Fahan and Inch Presbyterian Church on the Innishowen Peninsula.

Joseph Rhea was a scholarly man, well versed in philosophy, theology and the Hebrew and Latin languages, and he was spoken off as one of the most eminent clerics in the north of Ireland, and later in the frontier lands of America. Large in stature, he was six feet in height, with a cheerful disposition, full of Irish jokes; pleasant in manner and kind and charitable to a fault. He had been known to take off his shirt and give it to the needy.

He resigned his post at Fahan and Inch on August 16, 1769 after a disagreement over his annual salary of £24. His resignation to the congregation read:

"As I received the congregation of Fahan from the Presbytery of Londonderry, I have labored in the work of the ministry above twenty years in that place and as the congregation has fallen into very long areas and has been very deficient in the original promise to me which was 24 pounds yearly I am unable to subsist any longer among them and I do hereby demit my charge of them and deliver them into the hand of them from whom I received them.

Subscribed this 16th August, 1769.

JOSEPH REA

P.S. - I have only this further to request of the Presbytery that they will see justice done me in that congregation in my absence."

On September, 1769 he sailed from Londonderry in Lough Foyle to America with his wife Elizabeth McIlwaine and seven children - John, Matthew, Margaret, William, Joseph, Elizabeth and Samuel. His wife Elizabeth McIlwaine came from Lisfannin in Co. Donegal and another son James was born in America.

Joseph Rhea preached at Piney Creek near Taneytown in Maryland for four years on an annual salary of £112, which then equalled the sum of 560 dollars. He took a call to the Appalachian frontier in 1775 and it is believed he became only the second Presbyterian cleric to minister in the region we know of today as Tennessee.

The Rev. Charles Cummings, another minister of Scots-Irish descent, was the first and it was at the Holston River settlement in North Carolina (today North-East Tennessee) that he was joined by Rhea, who had left his family behind in Maryland to witness for Christ on the frontier. During his time on the Holston, Rhea joined up as a chaplain to the patriot troops of Colonel William Christian (another of Ulster-Scots tradition) for a four-week engagement against the Cherokee Indians on the Little Tennessee River.

It was said that Rhea, a gifted preacher and by then a man of 60, embraced every opportunity of preaching to the settlers in their wilderness homes and forts, and to the soldiers during his short time with them. Rhea, accompanied by his eldest son John, purchased lands at Beaver Creek in 1777 and he decided that he must return to Maryland to prepare the other members of the family for the wagon train trek to the new lands on the frontier. Sadly, after selling his property in Maryland, Joseph Rhea took ill with pneumonia and died, aged 62. He was buried in Piney Creek cemetery, Maryland.

A translation of a letter (in Latin) written by the Rev. Joseph Rhea to his son John on April 19, 1777 not only highlighted the dangers for the settlers on the frontier, but carried a prophetic message only five months from his death.

"I am well in body, but anxious in mind. The people of the Holston are in distress again on account of the savages. I hear that those in the fortifications below the hills are very numerous. I think that they will not have a spring harvest; the fate of them will be that they will not be able to live on that section. I sold my farm and I move not later than 5th June. If the Holston people do not about that time send two wagons for my family I shall, God willing, conduct them myself. I have now no place in which to put my family. I do not dispair, but I now think I was too hasty in selling my farm. Nothing in this world is done in vain, nothing accidentally, but all things by the omnipotent power. I beg you to write me; counsel and care for your brother Matthew. Mother and all the others at home are very well. I wrote you by Captain Thompson. This letter goes in the care of Captain Boyer, of Virginia, and from the home of Chiliaribi McAlister and from the town of that name. May you both live mindful of the future and conduct yourselves in a proper manner (as is becoming). So shun women and wine. You know that these have brought ruin to very many. Live soberly, secure the love of all men especially of the leader. I hope that God will guide me. I have made a mistake in selling my farm too hastily, but I trust that the Ruler of the world will bring me to a good end. That God will be with you and be a protection to you is the prayer of your most loving father".

Joseph Rhea's widow Elizabeth, her eldest son John and the rest of the family carried out his wish of removing to the Holston and after a hazardous six-week journey they reached their new home in the middle of a snowstorm in February, 1778.

The Rheas were followed to the Holston and Watauga regions of North Carolina by other Scots-Irish settlers who had been members of Joseph Rhea's congregation at Piney Creek. They were joined by friends from Virginia, and together they formed a settlement at the Holston Fork and a church called New Bethel, where they were ministered to by a contemporary of Joseph Rhea, the Rev. Samuel Doak. Among the names of the families who moved were Allison, Anderson, Breden, Hodges, Dysart, McAllister, McCorkle and Lynn.

The 2,000-acre Rhea farm on the Holston near what is now the town of Blountville was the scene of some of the earliest religious services in Tennessee. Joseph Rhea and Samuel Doak preached from a pulpit stone on the farm and portions of the old rock remain to this day. The large field behind the Rhea house served as training grounds for the   militia before the Revolutionary War and both Presidents Andrew Jackson and Andrew Johnson were frequent guests of the family. The farm was also used by the Confederate forces during the Civil War. Of the direct descendants of the Rev. Joseph Rhea, 21 became ministers of the gospel - Presbyterians, with a single exception and 54 were soldiers in the Confederate Army during the Civil War from 1861-65.

John Rhea born in the parish of Langhorn near Londonderry in 1753, was like his father a leader in his frontier community and he served with the patriot army at the Battle of Kings Mountain and Brandywine. He was clerk of the county court of Sullivan County when it became part of the ill-fated state of Franklin and was later in North Carolina; was a member of the House of Commons of North Carolina; a delegate from Sullivan County to the constitional convention of Tennessee in 1796; attorney general of Greene County, Tennessee; a member of the American Congress for 18 years and a United States commissioner in the treaty talks with the Choctaw Indians in 1816. He was a graduate of Princeton and after studying law was admitted to the bar in 1789. He was a leading educationalist in Tennessee and served for many years as trustee on the state's leading colleges - Greeneville, Washington and East Tennessee.

John Rhea was a strict Calvinist and had planned to become a Presbyterian minister. He was taken on trials by the Hanover Presbytery in Tennessee, but was never licensed or ordained. As a United States Congressman in 1812 he presented a petition from Christian denominations in the western part of the United States against the mail service being operated on a Sunday. The Government ruled that the daily transportation of the mails was a public necessity. Rhea, who never married, was a Democrat of the Thomas Jefferson school and a staunch friend of Andrew Jackson. In 1823 he retired from politics and died in Sullivan County in 1832. He is buried in Blountville, one of the oldest towns in Tennessee, a place where Scots-Irish families like the Rheas, Andersons, Maxwells, Rutledges and Tiptons settled.

It is known that John Rhea returned to Ireland in 1785 and brought to America, landing at New Castle, Delaware, a relative Mrs Elizabeth Dysart Breden, the widow of John Breden (Braden). She had eight children and three of her daughters married three of John Rhea's brothers and a fourth daughter married a cousin. Congressman or "Old John" Rhea, as he was often referred to, acquired large tracts of land in Tennessee and he became a very wealthy man for his times. He was partial to white horses and his journeys to Washington were always on a trusted steed, of that colour.

John's brother Matthew, born in Co.Donegal in 1755, was a lieutenant in the sixth Virginia Regiment of the Continental Army during the Revolutionary War and was at the battle of Guildford Courthouse in North Carolina. He was presented with a sword by General Nathaniel Green for gallantry in that battle. The sword was lost in battle by Lieutenant Matthew Rhea, great grandson of Rev. Joseph Rhea during the American Civil War. Matthew Sen's two sons Joseph M. and Robert P. Rhea were also soldiers of distinction. Both fought in the war of 1812 and were taken captive at Quebec in Canada. Robert P. was a school teacher in Virginia and one of his pupils was General "Stonewall" Jackson, who was of Ulster stock from the Birches in Co. Armagh.

Matthew Rhea (1795-1870), son of Matthew Sen. and grandson of Rev. Joseph Rhea, published in 1832 the first map of Tennessee, based on actual land surveys. This was considered a major contribution to early life in Tennessee. Matthew was married to Mary Looney, of a Scots-Irish pioneer family from Sullivan County. The couple lived in Maury County and in Middle Tennessee and Fayette County in Western Tennessee. They had 13 children.

Hill McAlister, the Governor of Tennessee in 1933-37, was a descendant from the Rhea-Breden-Dysart families and many other Tennessean luminaries of the 19th and 20th centuries orginated from this illustrious Scots-Irish line.

* Fahan and Inch Presbyterian Churches in Co. Donegal today belong to the Derry and Strabane Presbytery of the Presbyterian Church in Ireland. Fahan and Inch are only a short distance from Londonderry, Northern Ireland's second city.

CAMP MEETINGS

The Camp meeting was a unique phenomenon of religion in the Appalachian states almost 200 years ago. Started in Kentucky around 1800, the camp meetings became a vehicle of civilisation, conversion, and social interaction in what was seen as "a coarse, Godless life" in the American wilderness and in Tennessee they became very popular.

The camp meeting was more than a religious gathering. It was a social event for which folks travelled great distances. Most meetings lasted five to seven days and travellers had to bring supplies for a lengthy stay. There, people bartered for goods, traded and raced their horses, argued politics, and became acquainted with their neighbours. There too, men and women observed frontier courting rituals and many marriages began at the camp meeting. The songs and shouting, the unity of common meals and common prayer created a bond which was vital to the development of society on the frontier.

Religion was the dominant factor, however, and as the camp meeting became institutionalised, it became an important part of the religious life of the Appalachian states. Those converted in earlier camp meetings returned year after year to renew the original zeal of brighter days and stronger faith. The camp meetings soon became homecomings when the people of God, spread out across the mountains, came together to rekindle the fires of faith and strengthen the bonds of friendship.

Over a period, many of the early camp meeting sites became permanent camps as land was set aside for the perpetual use of the faithful. The Methodists were particularly active in the establishment of permanent camp meeting sites. Indeed, by the 19th century, Methodists had become the chief proponents of the camp meeting experience in America.

Today, camp meetings usually are organised around a schedule similar to that of the early frontier years. There are few activities beyond preaching, worship, and visiting with friends, revolving around a series of services from morning to night, divided by meals and an afternoon rest period. Services are presided over by the camp pastor but a variety of preachers are called upon to speak at the services.

Congregational participation continues to be important in modern camp meetings. Singing is loud and enthusiastic. Sermons urge conversion on the unsaved but also stress the responsibility of those already converted to grow in faith and Christian maturity. Invitations or "altar calls" are usually given at the end of each service in order to provide prayer and counselling for those seeking spiritual comfort.

Throughout the week there is also a sense of community as friendships are renewed and Christian fellowship shared among all who are present. Tears are shed, prayers are offered, and faith is renewed. The camp meeting continues to be an important time of religious and social rejuvenation among many Christian groups in Appalachia.

17

Families *who blazed a trail on the frontier*

THE ALEXANDERS

Various strands of this family moved from the north of Ireland during the 18th century, including a George Alexander who settled in Lancaster County, Pennsylvania in 1745.

George and his wife Jane had 10 sons and a daughter, and all 10 sons are listed as Revolutionary War soldiers in North Carolina. Captain William Alexander served with the 4th North Carolina Regiment and in 1797 he moved with his family to Greene County, Tennessee.

Eight Alexanders are listed as patriots at the Battle of Kings Mountain: Aiken Alexander, Daniel Alexander, Elias Alexander, Jeremiah Alexander, John Alexander, Oliver Alexander, James Alexander, from Rowan County, North Carolina, and Joseph Alexander, who was born in Co. Antrim in 1759 and lived at Spartanburg, South Carolina. It has not been firmly established their relation to one another, but obviously there must have been some family ties.

THE ARMSTRONGS

The Fermanagh Armstrongs were also associated with the Presbyterian settlement at Tinkling Springs, after emigrating from Ulster between 1730 and 1750. Brookeborough is the township they left in Fermanagh and the family tree can be traced back to the lowlands of Scotland in the 17th century.

Today, Armstrong is a very common name in Augusta County, Virginia and in East Tennessee, many of the clan probably tracing their ancestry back to William Armstrong, who was born in Fermanagh in 1712 and who lived in Hawkins County, Tennessee, to the advanced age of 103.

The New Providence Presbyterian Church, the oldest church in Tennessee in continuous existance from 1780, was founded in the home of William Armstrong, whose wife was Mary Caldwell from Ireland. A second William Armstrong is recorded as having served at the Battle of Kings Mountain, the Battle of Cowpens and was at Charleston when the British left. He is listed as born in Ireland in 1765.

Another Armstrong family, headed by Robert and Alice Calhoun, left Ulster in 1735 and, after staying in Pennsylvania for seven years, headed in the direction of South Carolina. Robert I never made the full journey to the frontier - he died at Augusta County, Virginia in 1754, but his children carried on eventually settling at Abbeville, South Carolina. Robert II was a lieutenant in the 1st South Carolina Regiment during the Revolutionary War and in 1784 was living in Washington County, North Carolina (today Tennessee).

His final home was five miles east of Knoxville on the Holston / French Broad Rivers. A nephew Robert Houston (son of Alice Armstrong) was the first sheriff of Knox County and later was Tennessee Secretary of State under Governors William Blount and John Sevier and a state senator.

Robert Houston, described as tall, muscular and a graceful man, had energy, thrift and intelligence, common to his Scots-Irish kinsfolk. He later became paymaster to the East Tennessee troops and was commissioner in the treaty completed with the Cherokees, the brainchild of John C. Calhoun, the then Secretary of War. John C's grandfather Patrick Calhoun was a brother of Robert Armstrong I's wife Alice.

The descendants of James Armstrong, another family bearing the name, were extensive farmers in Orange County, North Carolina from the first settlement there in the 1750s.

James (1701-1796) was Ulster-born and moved to Pennsylvania in the first wave of the Scots-Irish. He married Mollie Bird and they had six children. In 1755 Armstrong purchased 607 acres of land in Orange County for £29-12-0 (twenty nine pounds twelve shillings) and later extended his holdings with more purchases.

William Armstrong, a son married Jane Lapsley, of Scots-Irish stock from Virginia, and after his wife's death took a commission as ensign with the 1st North Carolina Battalion in the Revolutionary Army and rose to the rank of captain through service in the various battles. He received a land grant of 3,840 acres in Davidson County, now in middle Tennessee, which after a period of years, was sold and he finished his days in Hawkins County, East Tennessee.

THE CALDWELLS

Both William Armstrong and William Rutledge married Caldwell wives from Ireland. They are believed to have been sisters, for Augusta County records confirm that William and Thomas Rutledge, James Armstrong and James Caldwell had adjoining lands and they along with a William Armstrong played leading roles in the Tinkling Springs Church.

One research tells us that the Caldwells were an Ayrshire, Scotland family who moved to Ulster about 1650. They lived in Counties Fermanagh, Cavan, Londonderry and Donegal and the first of them to emigrate to America came in via the port of New Castle in Delaware in 1727. By 1734, they had reached the valley of Virginia.

THE CARMICHAELS

This family were leading Confederates in Tennessee during the American Civil War, operating in Davidson, White and Williamson Counties. They were descended from brothers John H. and Archibald Carmichael, Presbyterian stock who were born in Co. Antrim in the 1780s.

They were taken to America by their parents Thomas and Mary when only small boys and spent most of their early years in Orange County, North Carolina. Members of the family moved to Tennessee about 1830. Four brothers - Thomas, Hence, Solomon, and William L., sons of John H. Carmichael, were killed in the Civil War while serving in Confederate colours.

THE CAVINS

Presbyterian missionary Samuel Cavin left Belfast in 1737 and after landing in Philadelphia he became pastor of Spring Creek Church at Mechanicsburn, Pennsylvania.

Cavin died in 1750 and his descendants moved south, settling first in Iredell County, North Carolina. They followed Daniel Boone across the mountains into East Tennessee and set up homes in Washington and Hawkins counties in the north east of the state. Some of the Cavins live in this region today - others spread out to Middle Tennessee (Lebanon and Franklin) and west (Weakley County).

THE CHRISTIANS

Gilbert Christian, one of the heroic officers of the Revolutionary War, was the son and grandson of Ulster Presbyterians who left Ireland for Virginia in 1732. Grandfather Gilbert (born 1678) and his wife Elizabeth Margaret Richardson (born 1702 in Ireland) settled in Augusta County. Their son Robert, who was also born in Ireland, was recruiting officer for the militia in the county during the Revolution.

Gilbert II, won his captain's stripes while commanding the Sullivan County Militia and gained significant repute as an Indian fighter. He was in the front line at the Battle of Kings Mountain, was promoted to major and eventually colonel during expeditions to quell Indian unrest. He was a justice of the peace in Sullivan County and his son Robert married the daughter of John Adair, the Co. Antrim man who raised the money to arm the Battle of Kings Mountain forces.

THE CLARKS (CLARKES)

The Clarks of Pickett County in North Tennessee can trace their Scots-Irish link back to Henry Alexander Clark, who was born in Newry, Co. Down and emigrated to Virginia in the early 18th century. He was the son of William Richard and Mary Elizabeth Rogers Clark, who lived in Newry.

According to family sources, Clark "lived by his wits and his fists and survived" and is recorded in 1749 as being a chain-carrier for a young George Washington, then a surveyor in Virginia. When Washington was made colonel of the Virginia Militia, Henry Clark was his orderly sergeant and they made frequent trips across the Blue Ridge Mountains for surveying expeditions and to engage the French and the Indians.

The Clark family had been close neighbours of George Washington's parents, Augustine and Mary, when they lived in the Ferry Farm area of Westmorland County in Eastern Virginia. Henry Clark married English-born Amelia Stafford and they had three sons - William, Robert and James, all of whom served in the Revolutionary War under General George Washington. For his services in the War, Clark was awarded a land grant in Tennessee, but he was too old to make the journey by covered wagon from Virginia and sent his three sons instead to settle in Pickett County on the Cumberland Mountain plateau. A settlement was created in an area known today as Clark Mountain and out of a wilderness there quickly followed a Presbyterian Church and a school.

The Rev. Thomas Clark, a Scottish-born Presbyterian cleric who ministered at Ballybay in Co. Monaghan, led 300 emigrants from Newry to New York in 1764. Most of these people settled in Virginia.

In the post-Revolutionary period, two Clarke brothers John and Samuel from Killead in Co. Antrim emigrated to America in the 1790s. John engaged in commerce in Augusta, Georgia and when he died in 1822 he had an estate valued at over one million dollars. He was a member of First Presbyterian Church in Augusta.

THE CULBERTSONS

This Co. Antrim family provided more officers to the Revolutionary Army than any other family settled along the American frontier. The Culbertsons of Ballygan near Ballymoney were of ancient Scottish ancestry, and had been in Ulster since the early 17th century.

In 1730 three brothers - Alexander, Joseph and Samuel Culbertson, from near Ballymoney, emigrated to Lancaster County, Pennsylvania. They settled in Lurgan, Franklin County, and called their settlement "Culbertson's Row", after the home of their ancestors in Ulster.

During the mid-1750s the Culbertsons migrated down the Great Wagon Road to South Carolina and there the families of James, Joseph, Josiah and Samuel spread out. Josiah served as a major and Samuel as a lieutenant and captain at the Battles of Kings Mountain and Cowpens. Robert and Joseph Culbertson, also listed at Kings Mountain, were engaged in the various Indian Wars.

THE DITTYS

John Ditty was a Revolutionary War veteran who moved to Tennessee with his family after a few years of settlement in Virginia. This son

of Ulster-born parents was a blacksmith by trade and during the war he
served with the Lancaster unit of the Pennsylvania Militia.

When the War ended John lived at Berwick in Pennsylvania, but by
1797 he was running a tavern at Christianburn, Montgomery County,
Virginia. Two years later, he was appointed road overseer in the same
county. John's next move was to Tennessee in the early 1800s and it
was near the town of Cookeville that he carried on a blacksmith's shop.
He died in 1846 aged 90. After this some members of the family moved
to new lands in Missouri and Oregon.

THE HAMILTONS

Captain Thomas Hamilton and his family blazed an illustrious trail
in the frontier lands around Nashville in 1780s/1790s, the years preceding the formation of the state of Tennessee. Thomas and his wife Jane
McCracken were both born in Ulster around 1725-30 and moved to
North Carolina via Pennsylvania in 1750 to start a family and a new
life. They had 10 children. After serving in the North Carolina militia in
the Revolutionary War, Hamilton moved to Mansker's Fort at
Goodlettsville, Tennessee - a pioneering station in an area largely occupied by Cherokee Indian tribes.

For a period Hamilton moved away from his family as he explored
the wilderness. At Tyree Springs Road (halfway between present-day
Hendersonville and Whitehouse close to Nashville) he lived in an Indian cave and in 1789 built a fort nearby, to which families would move
for safety when there was the threat of attack from the Cherokees. The
fort, known as Hamilton's station, stood until 1930.

His sons Thomas and James also served in the Revolutionary War,
with James figuring prominently at the Battle of Kings Mountain.
Thomas accompanied Andrew Jackson at the Battle of New Orleans in
1814. James Hamilton received a land grant on Stone's River close to
Nashville and lived close to Colonel John Donelson, whose daughter
Rachel married Andrew Jackson. Hamilton and Donelson served together in the North Carolina Militia. The Hamiltons were leading members of the Ridge and Cumberland Presbyterian Churches in the area.

THE HELMS

This family originated in Co. Tyrone and it was Moses Helms who
emigrated to America with his wife Sarah Jameson about 1740. They

were Presbyterian stock and had connections with the Steele, Carson and Porter families. Two members of the family, John and Meredith Helms, were soldiers at the Battle of Kings Mountain in 1780.

THE KENNEDYS

Seven Kennedys, of Scots-Irish Presbyterian stock, are listed as patriots at the Battle of Kings Mountain, the foremost being Captain Robert Kennedy and Captain Thomas Kennedy. The others were William, William Jun., John, Daniel and Moses.

The Ulster-born father of William Sen. came through the valley of Virginia from Augusta County to Union County, South Carolina and his sons and grandsons fought with distinction in the Revolutionary War. These Kennedys were cousins of the Campbells, 11 of whom were listed at Kings Mountain. Many of the family settled in the Holston area of East Tennessee.

Daniel Kennedy fought with Colonel Isaac Shelby in Lord Dunmore's War of 1774 and in 1776 he helped defend Fort Watauga from 500 Cherokee Indians during a siege which lasted 14 days. He settled on 4,000 acres at Little Limestone Creek, near where Davy Crockett was born. At Kings Mountain, Daniel Kennedy was in the frontal assault on Ferguson's troops and at the surrender he received the sword of one of the British officers. He later became clerk of Greene County Court; was involved in the establishment of the ill-fated state of Franklin and served in the North Carolina Assembly. He helped form Greene County and the Mount Zion Presbyterian Church there, and was a trustee of Greeneville and Washington Colleges.

The Rev. Samuel Kennedy was an Ulster-born Presbyterian minister who had a church at Williamsburg in South Carolina from 1782 and later moved to Mecklenburg, North Carolina. There was also a Presbyterian family of Kennedys who settled in Clarksville, Montgomery County, Tennessee, one of the earliest members being John F. Kennedy. (no relation of the later American President).

THE KIRKPATRICKS

Various strands of this family settled in Tennessee and the earliest known emigrant bearing the name was William Kirkpatrick, who was born in Co. Armagh in 1719 and settled in Lancaster county, Pennsylvania.

A John Hugh Kirkpatrick has his birthplace listed as Inverness in Scotland in 1741 and he may have lived in the north of Ireland before moving to America. He pioneered from Rockingham in Virginia and, with Daniel Boone, helped cut the Wilderness Road to the Watuaga district of North Carolina.

John Hugh led a wagon train to Bull's Gap in Tennessee in 1778 and established Salem, the first Presbyterian Church in the region. He was a hero of the Revolutionary War and four of his sons John, Jacob, Wilkins, and William were settlers of Jefferson County, Tennessee. His wife was Margaret Jane Wilkins. John Hugh was a near relative of Major Robert Kirkpatrick, who was killed in a battle with Indians at Louden under Colonel John Sevier.

Jacob Kirkpatrick was a soldier in the Indian wars and reared seven orphan children beside his own family of nine. His wife Isabella White was the daughter of a Baptist pastor who came to America at a very early date. In 1840 the state of Tennessee contained 57 Kirkpatrick households.

THE McFARLANDS

The earliest settlement in what was to become Hamblin County in north east Tennessee was known as the "Irish Bottom" due to the preponderance of settlers with those ties. This Nolichucky River region was first pioneered in 1783 by Robert McFarland, who had come from North Carolina and had been present at the Battle of Kings Mountain in 1780.

McFarland served as Sheriff of Jefferson County in Tennessee in 1792-1800 after earlier being a justice of the peace during the abortive attempt to organise the state of Franklin. His grandfather John and father Robert emigrated from Co. Antrim about 1746 and settled first in Augusta County, Virginia. Robert Sen. was a lieutenant in the militia in Augusta County, before moving to North Carolina, and Kentucky. The family were staunch Presbyterians, grandfather John being an elder in Augusta Old Church.

THE McJUNKINS AND McCHESNEYS

The McJunkins from Co. Tyrone and the McChesneys from Co. Antrim who moved to America in the mid-18th century were also formidable frontiersmen and their exploits are recorded with pride in the annals of Tennessee, the Carolinas and Kentucky.

Robert J. McJunkin and his wife Margaret Caldwell left Stewartstown in Co. Tyrone for Pennsylvania with his family in 1741, while the McChesney link in America begins with the movement of a family of 10 from the port of Larne in Co. Antrim to Charleston in South Carolina in 1772.

The McChesneys (they changed their name to Chesney when they landed in America) lost an eight-month-old baby from smallpox on the arduous 52-day journey across the Atlantic on the ship The James and Mary. But life had been hard on the small family farm at Dunclug (now in present-day Ballymena) and conditions in the new world just had to be tried.

The McJunkin/Chesney families became linked when Jane Chesney, who survived the smallpox scare on that fateful passage, married Revolutionary War hero Daniel McJunkin, a grandson of Robert J., from Stewartstown, Co. Tyrone. Samuel McJunkin, a son of Robert J., had moved to South Carolina with his wife Mary Anne Bogan, also of Ulster Presbyterian stock, and three of their sons distinguished themselves in the Revolutionary War.

By the time the War began, Samuel (born in Tyrone in 1725) was too old to serve, but for most of his life in America he was active in seeking the liberties of the settlers from the Crown and had engaged in many battles with the Indians. He had been an elder in the Presbyterian Church at Brown's Creek in Union County, South Carolina for 40 years and was a Justice of the Peace.

Major Joseph McJunkin, also an elder in the Presbyterian Church, fought throughout the Revolutionary War, while Daniel, a private and a horseman, is recorded as having served at the Battle of Kings Mountain in 1780. He was seriously injured during the War and was imprisoned for a time by the British. A third son Samuel Jun. also served.

Mary Anne McJunkin died of smallpox while attending the War wounded. Samuel Sen. died 30 years later in Kentucky while attempting to make the new Indiana territories with younger members of his family. The family of Daniel and Jane McJunkin moved to East Tennessee from South Carolina in 1819 and settled in Polk County. There are family connections there to this day. Jane's brother Alexander was a leading South Carolina loyalist throughout the Revolutionary War period and after and he returned to Ulster to trace his family roots, among the Purdys and Pedens of Clough and Glenravil in Antrim and Annalong in Co. Down and the McChesneys of Dunclug. The Journal of Alexander Chesney is a well-documented work on the Scots-Irish movement to America.

THE McKAUGHANS

This Ulster Presbyterian family began their American links about 1747 with the movement of Archibald McKaughan, his wife Rebecca and their two young sons Archibald Jnr (aged 12) and Hugh (age 4) from Co. Antrim. They settled at Cumberland County in Pennsylvania, where they lived for a number of years, and while there, two daughters Margaret and Rebecca, were born.

Both Archibald Sen. and his wife Rebecca Boyd were born about 1715 and married in 1733. Rebecca was the only child of Alexander Boyd, an Ulster merchant involved in the manufacture of glass. He lived at 'Glass Island', Co. Antrim, owning a manor house noted for its grandeur - a man of considerable wealth.

It was said that 50 years after his death, Irish lawyers went to America to see if they could ascertain a number of descendants of Rebecca Boyd McKaughan living there. They looked at North Carolina and Texas, but it is claimed they never looked to Tennessee nor Kentucky, where the offspring of Archibald and Rebecca were located.

Archibald Jnr. married a Jane Mercer and Hugh a Charlotte Blake and both men served against the British in the Revolutionary War. Along with the brothers of Jane Mercer, the two McKaughans were given land for war service from the Government in West Carolina (now Sullivan County in East Tennessee) and the McKaughan and Mercer clan prospered in the area. They cleared their land, built their cabins, in time made peace with the Indians and sowed their crops - the embryo of a typical frontier family.

Archibald Jnr. and the Mercer brothers moved to Pulaski County in Kentucky with their families. But Hugh and the rest of the McKaughans, including Rebecca Boyd McKaughan, moved to what is now Jackson County in Tennessee where she died at the age of 100 in 1816. She is buried at Rob Draper Cemetery in Gainsboro, Tennessee.

Joab Brooks, from Scott County, Arkansas, a great grandson of Rebecca Boyd McKaughan, related how his great grandmother told of being an heiress of Alexander Boyd, who died in Ireland. She also said that she married Archibald McKaughan near Belfast, Ireland contrary to her father's will; that she and her husband remained in that country (in and around Belfast) for some 14 years after their marriage and until their eldest son was about 12 years old, after which time a difficulty arose between her husband and her father which led to she and her husband coming to America.

"I learned from my great grandmother, Rebecca Boyd, that her father was the owner of a manor house near Belfast, Ireland, which was noted for its grandeur and often termed the 'Glass House', on account of part of the wall being solid mirror - at least this is the way I understand it from her statement," said Joab Brooks.

• McCaughan is a very common name in Co. Antrim today and it is believed to be derived from McKaughan, a surname which has now virtually died out in Northern Ireland.

THE McKEYS

A member of this Ulster-Scots family, who settled in East Tennessee in the early 19th century, became one of the leading newspaper editors in Indiana. He was Benjamin F. McKey, who edited and owned the Lebanon Pioneer for 34 years until 1924.

His great-grandparents Benjamin and Polly (Potter) McKey were both born in Co. Antrim of Scottish ancestry and lived in Greene County and Knoxville in Tennessee. A grandson, Jefferson C. McKey, Ben F's father, was a prominent farmer in Boone County, Indiana by the mid-19th century.

THE McKNIGHTS

This family who settled in Rowan County, North Carolina about the 1750 period came from Londonderry and travelled through the valley of Virginia from Pennsylvania. William McKnight moved from Ireland with his mother and sweetheart Jane Morton and when they married had a family of three sons James, William and David.

William McKnight, believed to be of the same family, served in the Battle of Kings Mountain and Musgrove's Mill in the colours of the South Carolina militia. He was born in Rowan County in 1761 and died in Lawrence County in Arkansas in 1844.

THE MURPHYS

Miles Murphy, born in the north of Ireland about 1725, was one of the first bearing this family name to reach the American frontier. He came of Protestant stock and was known to be living at Sampson County, North Carolina in 1790. Later members of the family moved to Bethel in Maury County, middle-Tennessee and belonged to the Christian Church there.

Nathaniel Murphy, son of Miles, married Mary "Polly" Mack, a daughter of John Mack, who, although Scottish-born, is believed to have arrived in America with his family from Ireland. Mack served with the 1st Virginia State Regiment in the Revolutionary War and he settled in both North Carolina and Virginia. Nathaniel Murphy lived in both Maury and Rutherford Counties in Tennessee and members of the family had gallant service for the Confederacy in the Civil War. The Murphys - Macks prospered in farming in middle-Tennessee and a number distinguished themselves in public life.

The son and six grandsons of Daniel Murphy who moved from the north of Ireland to Charles County in Maryland about 1710 were soldiers in the Revolutionary War. Daniel died soon after arriving in America, but when the call to arms came his son Daniel, known as Daniel Sen., and grandsons Daniel Jun., Abraham, Joseph, Zachariah, Zephaniah and Hezekiah responded. Hezakiah was wounded in action.

As their Old Testament names convey the Murphys were a strongly religious family, well-versed in the teachings of the Bible. Several generations of the family settled in Maryland, but later some members moved to Overton and Jackson counties in Tennessee.

THE RUTLEDGES

Members of this Co. Tyrone Presbyterian family were among the very first settlers in Tennessee after moving through the valley of

Virginia. Brothers William, Thomas and John and sisters Jane and Catherine left the home country in the mid-18th century and while some of the family took root in Augusta County, Virginia, others trekked on to that part of North Carolina which today is in Tennessee.

The most famous Rutledge was George, a brigadier general who succeeded John Sevier in the foremost Tennessee army position when Sevier became Tennessee's first Governor in 1796. This native-born Ulsterman was at the Battle of Kings Mountain and represented Sullivan County in the first Tennessee legislature and was a senator in the third. The county seat of Grainger County, Tennessee is named in his honour.

George Rutledge was married to Annis Armstrong, a member of a family who moved from Co. Fermanagh in the west of Ulster. William Rutledge, General George's father, set up home at Tinkling Springs in Augusta County, Virginia and there he married Eleanor Caldwell, who was born in Co. Cavan, Ireland.

The Rutledges were prominent members at the Tinkling Springs Presbyterian meeting house, but when land became available in North Carolina in 1777 they set off in hot pursuit. By 1783 they had acquired a land grant of 450 acres at the Holston River region, now Sullivan County in East Tennessee.

THE SLATERYS

Patrick Slatery owned 800 acres of land in Knox County in East Tennessee in the 1790s called "Slatery's Mountain" and was a close confidante of Sam Houston and Tennessee's first Governor John Sevier.

It is believed Patrick Slatery's family were originally Irish Roman Catholics, but descendants joined the Protestant faith and were heavily involved in a number of Reformed churches in Tennessee. Patrick's children married into the Houston, Kennedy, Mikels and Coulson families. Patrick had been in the New York Militia in the 1770s soon after his arrival in America and served in the Revolutionary War. He ran a grist mill in East Tennessee in the years leading up to the formation of the state.

18

Scots-Irish *in the Revolutionary War*

JOHN McCANDLESS

Co. Down man John McCandless was drafted into military service within three years of his arrival in America and served with distinction throughout the Revolutionary War. John, born in 1750, sailed from Belfast to New Castle, Delaware on June 5, 1772, arriving on August 26. He resided in Baltimore for a few months and moved to Mecklenburg county in North Carolina.

On his first military assignment he served under Colonel Thomas Polk, a forebear of President James K. Polk, and Major James White, the founder of Knoxville. He rose from being a wagoner to a mounted horseman and went into action against the British in several key battles. McCandless moved to Tennessee in 1799, living in Blount County and then Maury County, where he finished his days living on a Revolutionary War pension of 23.33 dollars a year. He was close on 90 when he died.

JOHN McCRORY

This Ulsterman arrived in America with his family in 1775 when he was 12 and lived at Guildford County in North Carolina. He joined the Revolutionary militia at 18 and among his first duties was guarding Tory officers, Americans who were loyal to the British. McCrory got a sick discharge near the end of the war and he lived in Maury county in Tennessee from 1830, living off a 40-dollar per year war pension.

SMITH WILLIS

This American Revolutionary soldier was born in Co. Antrim in 1764 and taken to Pennsylvania with his family when a small boy. Smith Willis became a militia soldier when only 15 and was drafted immediately into the wars with the British and the Indians on the friontier.

Willis lived at Northampton, Pennsylvania, then moved to York County in the same state and when he went to live in Washington County in Virginia he married Mary McMullan, who also came of Scots-Irish stock. The couple lived in Wayne County, Kentucky for some years, then Morgan County in East Tennessee. Mary Willis died in 1828 and Smith re-married in 1836. He died in 1849, aged 85 - a Revolutionary War soldier on a pension of 20 dollars a year.

Elizabeth Willis, daughter of Smith and Mary Willis married William Guffey, a Virginian of Scottish ancestory who served in the Indian Wars of 1812-13 as a private in the First Regiment Tennessee Volunteers. Members of the Willis-Guffey connnection later served in the American Civil War in the 1860s. One William Riley Davis, a great grandson of Smith Willis and William Guffey, fought for the Union cause as a private in the 8th Regiment Tennessee Infantry.

HUGH ROGAN

Roman Catholic Hugh Rogan differed in faith from the vast majority of the early American settlers but he stood manfully alongside the Scots-Irish Presbyterians in opening up the new frontier lands.

Hugh was a native of Glentoran in Co. Donegal who moved from Ireland to Pennsylvania in 1776 on the eve of the Revolutionary War and headed West to North Carolina with two other Irish Roman Catholics Daniel and Thomas Carlin, Rogan settled for several years, living happily with fellow countrymen of the Presbyterian faith. All three saw service in the Revolutionary War and the store they ran at Hornet's Nest in North Carolina was known as the "Catholic" store.

Rogan was a member of John Donelson's party who first settled Fort Nashborough (Nashville) in 1780 and he was a signator of the

Cumberland Compact, the first instrument of government in middle Tennessee. For 20 years he defended the forts and settlements in the region against the Indians.

He built a two-room stone cottage alongside 640 acres of land in what is now Sumner County in middle Tennessee and this building became a rare surviving example of early Irish folk housing as it was adapted to the lifestyle of Tennessee.

Rogan left behind a wife and baby son when he emigrated from Ireland and 20 years was to elapse before he managed to return to Donegal for a reunion. At first his wife did not know him, as 20 years of a harsh existence on the frontier had aged him considerably. But they became reconciled and with their 21-year-old son Bernard headed across the Atlantic to the home he had prepared in Sumner County. Another son Francis was born to the couple in 1798 and Hugh died in 1812, a prosperous and highly respected member of the community in this part of Tennessee.

Hugh Rogan and his family helped establish the Roman Catholic Church in Sumner County, although for most of his time spent in America, Hugh had never seen a priest. His son Francis was not baptised until he was over 30, so scarce were priests in that part of Tennessee. But Hugh Rogan, like his Presbyterian neighbours, managed to hold on firmly to the faith he had been born into back in his native Ireland.

19

Movement *to South Carolina*

South Carolina was a region tens of thousands of Ulster Scots set
tled in during the 18th century and many of these stout Presbyterians moved on to the neighbouring state of Tennessee and further west to the frontier lands of Kansas and Missouri. Whole congregations lifted their roots in the hills of Co. Antrim and headed to the
Carolinas, so penalised were they by the strictures of iniquitous absen-
tee landlords who kept hounding them for rents from the meagre Irish
farmlands.

The lot of the Presbyterian people in the north of Ireland in the mid-
18th century was not a happy one. Not only were they being asked to
pay taxes to a church (the Episcopal Church of Ireland) which was not
their own and rents that were far beyond their financial resources, but
the textile industry and agriculture they were employed in had hit hard
times. Money was scarce among the small landholders.

The plight was illustrated by the attempted eviction from their homes
of members of a Covenanting congregation (Reformed Presbyterian) in
Ballymoney, Co. Antrim about 1772 which forced the minister the Rev.
William Martin to declare to his people in a sermon on the following
Sunday morning that "enough was enough".

William Martin said that anyone who knew anything about the Ulster countryside realised that the rents were so high that the land would
not bring in enough to pay them. "Many of us are beggared and in time
all would be", he said, making it clear that as a minister he could not
stand idly by and await the violence and ruin that would come.

"Steps should be taken now to see that such situations did not develop", he declared, proposing that they all pool their resources and send to Belfast to charter ships for emigration to South Carolina where they would obtain free land and live as free men.

The Ballymoney congregation, having nothing to lose, agreed unanimously. They left with other Covenanters in five ships: The James and Mary, Lord Dunluce, Pennsylvania Farmer, Hopewell and the Free Mason and on the voyage of seven to nine weeks the destination was the port of Charleston in South Carolina. In all, 467 families travelled on the five ships in 1772. Names of the families included: Linn, Malcolm, Stephenson, Anderson, Caldwell, Clark, Gillespie, McAllister, McChesney, McCauley, Adams, Campbell, Fleming, McKay, Irvine, McCullough and McClure.

William Martin was the son of David Martin of Londonderry and he was born at Ballyspollum near Ballykee, Ballykelly in 1729. He was ordained as a minister of the Reformed Presbyterian Church at The Vow near Rasharkin in Co. Antrim in 1757 and was placed in charge of the nearby Ballymoney congregation.

With an education in theology from the University of Glasgow, Martin became active in establishing the Reformed "Covenanter" Presbyterian Church in Ireland and though congregations were scattered there were sufficient ministers by 1768 to form a Presbytery of Ireland. Martin was attached to Kellswater congregation outside Ballymena and it is recorded that "the Rev. William Martin (Kellswater)" was one of the agents who signed up the passengers for the Lord Dunluce ship, on which he sailed.

The first settlements in South Carolina were along the coast, where the economy was based on the rice plantations and the slave labour trade. But when the movement of Presbyterian Ulster-Scots ("poor Protestants" they were called by the colonists) started in 1730 the settlers were given land farther inland at a small rental.

By 1761, a bounty of £4 was being offered to "poor Protestants" from Europe to settle in the region, with smaller amounts paid to children. Ulster-Scots were among those who availed of this bounty, but when the offer was abolished in 1768 the South Carolina authorities ruled that the settlers were still entitled to their lands free of charge.

William and Barbara Chestnut Moffatt were a typical Covenanting couple who moved from Co. Antrim to South Carolina in the emigration wave of the autumn of 1772.

With their young son Samuel they sailed from Belfast to Charleston on the Mary Jane ship and upon arrival were given 500 acres of land at Little Rock Creek in Chester County. William served in the Revolutionary War, maintaining a tradition of a forebear Samuel Mophet of Ayr in Scotland, who was involved in the Covenanter uprising against King Charles II at Bothwell's Bridge in 1679. The Moffatts belonged to Ballylig Reformed Presbyterian Church in the parish of Rathcavin, which is in the area of the present-day Co. Antrim village of Broughshane.

The Rev. William Martin and his Covenanters from Ballymoney settled on lands that were given free. It was not only Covenanters who made the long journey from Co. Antrim to South Carolina: members of the Seceders, a splinter Presbyterian group, left the Ballyreshane, Derrykeghen, Ballymoney and Kilraughts areas. There were also Associate Presbyterians and Presbyterians who went under the title of Burghers and Anti-Burghers. Some had come via Pennsylvania.

On arrival in South Carolina these Calvinistic groups combined to build a union church at Rocky Mountain Road, 15 miles from the town of Chester. This church was called "Catholic" and it was there that the Rev. William Martin received a call. For several years Martin preached at "Catholic", until his own Covenanting people withdrew and built their own log church on a spot two miles further on.

The Revolutionary War was being fought in America at the time and the Presbyterian settlers in South Carolina were caught up in the conflict. William Martin, not forgetting why he and his flock had to leave Ireland, made clear from the pulpit his trenchant views on the British and the Tories.

He reminded his congregation of the hardships their fathers had suffered, in religion and in their possessions: "they had been forced out of Scotland; had been forced out of Ireland, had come over to America and cleared their lands and homes and their church and were free men". He warned that the British were coming in and soldiers would again be depriving them of the fruits of their labours and would be driving them out. They should not stand, he said, meekly and idly by while all they had wrought was taken from them. "There was a time to pray and a time to fight and the time to fight had come".

After the service two companies of militiamen were formed. The next day they set off with arms and horses to join the American forces attempting to repulse the British. William Martin's sermon, however, had reached the ears of British commanders and the church was burned down, he was arrested and confined to six months imprisonment.

On release, Martin turned to the congregation at Catholic and a split came in 1782 when other covenanting ministers Cuthbertson, Dobbin and Linn in Pennsylvania joined with other groups of Presbyterians to form the Associate Reformed Presbyterian Church. Martin stayed outside this grouping claiming he was the only Covenanter minister in America "who professed to teach the whole doctrine of the Reformation and who kept alive the Covenanter Church of America".

By this time, William Martin, unfortunately, had taken to drink and in 1785 he was dismissed by the Catholic congregation for his intemperance. Controversy raged whether this fiery Ulsterman drunk to excess or whether he was merely accepting "treats" at various houses that he called on during visitations.

His preaching continued, with meetings held in school houses, and when Reformed Church ministers the Rev. James McGarragh, from Ireland, and the Rev. William King, from Scotland, arrived as missionaries in the region they teamed up with Martin to establish a Reformed Presbytery.

Martin had a new church built at Rocky Mountain Road and, while his alliance with McGarragh and King lasted only a few years, he remained faithful to his congregation until he died in 1806, as a result of injury by a fall from his horse.

Whatever the Rev. William Martin's addiction to alcohol in his later years he is looked back on as "a proficient scholar, an eloquent preacher and an able divine". Preaching the gospel as a Christian minister could not have been easy in the Co. Antrim hillsides and the South Carolina frontier lands of the 18th century, realising the discriminatory laws that were enforced against non-conformist groups like the Covenanters.

THE CUMBERLAND GAP

The Cumberland Gap - the pivotal crossing point which pulls together the states of Tennessee, Kentucky and Virginia - was a well-worn path for the Scots-Irish who pioneered the region 200 years ago. It was through the Gap that the great wagon trains carrying the settlers moved to the rich bluegrass pastures of Kentucky and where frontiersman Daniel Boone stood like a beacon pointing his people towards the new lands. For centuries before the European settlers arrived the Cumberland Gap was used by Indian tribes as access to hunting grounds in Kentucky, Tennessee and Ohio.

Dr. Thomas Walker, in 1750, is credited with being the first white man to come across the Gap and he eagerly mapped out the location, because until then the early colonists found progress across the high-peaked Allegheny Mountains to new lands in Tennessee and Kentucky a real stumbling block.

Thomas Walker named the Cumberland mountain range, river and gap after the Duke of Cumberland, son of King George II. Walker was a Virginian of Scottish descent. Within 20 years Daniel Boone was on the scene, with others forging a way through for the settlers. Daniel, of Quaker stock from Exeter in the south west of England, first sighted the Cumberland Gap in 1769 after leaving his North Carolina farm with five hunting and scouting companions.

After descending the western side of the Appalachian mountain range, Boone and companions marvelled "from the top of an eminence, the beautiful level of Kentucke", a fertile land of cane and clover. After several trips through the Gap he returned in 1775 with about 30 woodsmen and with their axes they felled a road through the forest. The frontier had been opened up to Kentucky, Tennessee and Ohio by virtue of Boone's Wilderness Road.

By 1800, it is estimated that three-quarters of the settlers moving to the frontier lands, a very big percentage of them Scots-Irish, had made it there through the Cumberland Gap along the Wilderness Road.

Before the Revolutionary War an estimated 12,000 had crossed the Gap into the new frontier and by June 1, 1792, when Kentucky became a state of the Union, more than 100,000 people had passed through the 300-feet plain above a valley floor. It was a high-risk route for the settlers, for there was always the danger of attack from Cherokee and Shawnee Indians and from renegades and marauders.

By 1800, the Gap was used for transportation and commerce from east to west and today it still acts as a link between Tennessee, Kentucky and Virginia. In 1862-63 during the Civil war the Union Army used the Gap as the route into Tennessee.

Geologically the Gap is the result of dynamic earth stresses and movements from a bygone age. The north side of the Cumberland Mountain is of sandstone, shales and conglomerates, while the south side is of limestone which is said to contribute to the spectacular scenary and sheer cliffs. Many families settled in the plains close to the Gap and today the region is encapsuled into an American National Park, preserving the great heritage of both the Revolutionary War period and the Civil War.

The Gap was known as "the keystone" of the Confederacy and the Gibraltar of America. Both the Confederate and Union Armies believed the invasion of the North or the South would come through the Gap and from the two sides they fortified the Gap against an invasion which never came.

20

Conflict *with the Indians*

The fierce Scots-Irish conflict with the Indian tribes on the Ameri can frontier 200 years ago was nowhere more pronounced than in Maury County. The rich fertile lands of this middle-Tennessee region were used by the Indians as hunting ground and when the settlers moved in there was a deeply-felt resentment by the tribes which split over into savage blood-letting. Indians had never lived in the area, preferring to reside to the east and west and to hunt the buffalo, bear and elk which roamed freely close by.

After the Revolutionary War, American soldiers were rewarded for their services, not with money, but with generous land grants in the settlements of North and South Carolina and in the areas that today are in Tennessee.

Surveyors were sent in to draw up the new land boundaries and the grants to each soldier depended on rank: a private received 640 acres, a captain 3,840 and a brigadier general up to 12,000.

General Nathaniel Greene was given 25,000 acres of "best lands" in middle-Tennessee in 1783 and despite the hostility of the Chickasaw, Cherokee and Chawnee Indians the settlement of Maury County - officially established in 1807 - began to take shape, with hundreds of Scots-Irish families in the first wave.

A tombstone in a disused cemetery off the main street in Columbia, the Maury County capital, highlights the kind of dangers the settlers faced when they first arrived. Shawnee Indians struck on May 9, 1788 at the family homestead of James and Jane Gillespie Brown just off the

Tennessee River. James's head was cut from his body and dumped in the river and two of his sons were also killed. The surviving members of the family, his wife, other sons and daughters were taken captive.

One son was held for five years, another for 17 months and Jane Brown and one of her daughters were forced to march hundreds of miles barefoot to Ohio. They managed to return to Maury and the county's first court was held in the log cabin home of a son Joseph.

Jane Brown lived in Columbia until her death in 1831 and on her tombstone in the disused cemetery the story of the family's ordeal is related, providing a very telling reminder: "The reason I tell you these things O reader is so you will know at what cost this liberty which you enjoy today was won for you". The conflict between the settlers and the Indians over land was fuelled when several of the tribes sided with the British and French colonialists and the Indian tribes were instantly seen as the enemy.

A few months before the Brown attack, surveyors Captain William Pruett, Moses Brown and Daniel Johnson were massacred by Indians, but these and other attacks were speedily avenged. In one, James Robertson, one of the heroes of the Battle of Kings Mountain and a founder of Nashville, led a raid on an Indian village Coldwater in Alabama, destroying the village. During this attack a young William Pillow, later to settle in Maury County, killed a noted Indian chief Big Foot.

In another incident, leading frontiersman Colonel Anthony Bledsoe was killed by Indians. He lingered in agony for several hours and in his last moments drew up a will ensuring that his daughters could inherit his property in Sumner County.

The Indian attacks in the region were at their bloodiest during the 1790s. This was primarily due to the ferocity of a Cherokee chief Doublehead, who personally led murderous attacks on the white settlements from a base in Alabama. His route lay through Maury County and the raids were so numerous that one road became known as Doublehead Trace.

In July, 1793 Nathaniel Teal, a mail carrier between Nashville and Natchez, was killed by Indians hunting at Cathey's Creek, but matters came to a head when the Indian village of Nickajack was destroyed in 1794 by Colonel James Robertson and his group of militia. Robertson's group was piloted to the village by James Brown, who remembered the route from the days of his captivity in 1788.

Terrible atrocities were committed on both sides in the struggle for the lands of middle-Tennessee, but this part of America would never have been settled had it not been for the courage and determination of the early frontier families. People died and suffered greatly to take this rich wilderness and turn it into the country which today Americans love and enjoy so much. It was a land won at a cost and that cost came with the blood of native-born or first or second generation Irish men and women, Scots-Irish.

Though most of the settlers in the Maury County region were Scots-Irish, it was survival and advancement, rather than historical and religious ties, which bonded them together. There was more focus on what they were doing at that moment than where they had come from. The last Indian scalping was recorded in Maury County in 1804. By then, the region had become a viable and relatively safe area for the settlers.

One group of Ulster-Scots Presbyterians of Co. Down extraction arrived from Williamsburg in South Carolina in 1805 and formed the Zion community outside Columbia. Then in 1806, Dr. Gabriel Bumpass of Abbeyville district in South Carolina gathered together about 50 families and headed west. They reached Nashville, but finding the going difficult decided to leave the women and children at the fort there until land could be found and homes erected.

On the outskirts of Columbia they encountered canebrake as high as 25 feet, so a circuitous route was opened up and this became known as the Bumpass Trail. By 1808, the final destination had been reached, Dr. Bumpass and his friends stayed put. Numbered with them was George Newton, one of four brothers who had emigrated from Ulster to South Carolina. Family records claim that George reached Tennessee by ox cart, trekking over terrible mountainous paths.

The Newtons were related through marriage to the Ezell and Lucas families and today these names are to be found in sizeable numbers in middle Tennessee. The Ezells were of the Primitive Baptist faith and founded the first Baptist church in Giles County, Tennessee.

Unlike the pacifist Quakers in Pennsylvania who treated the Indians almost as friends and equals, the Scots-Irish settlers looked on the Indian tribes with deep suspicion and hostility. The Indians stood between them and the new lands of the frontier and as one side resisted the advance the other became more determined to push forward. If the Indians raided the settlements the settlers retaliated with a vengence, adopting the tactics of the native tribes.

The English, Quaker and German settlers stood back from a head-on clash with the Indians, but not so the Scots-Irish. They, more than any other race of white people, contributed to the ultimate defeat of the Indian tribes in the Appalachian frontier lands of America.

Death followed death on the frontier, very often away from the plains of warfare. Innocents on both sides suffered terribly, but as the white population increased dramatically all over the frontier states there was only going to be one winner and the proud Indian nations suffered great humiliation. Villages were laid bare as the native Americans were directed along the trails of tears to near oblivion in Oklahoma, Ohio and various points west.

Disease also played a part in decimating the Indian population - smallpox, rubella, tuberculosis and sexually transmitted epidemics took an horrendous toll.

Tens of thousands of Indians were forced off their lands and driven into exile. The rationale of the white settlers was that the native tribes were uncivilised and considered unworthy of holding on to the lands which they had lived on for hundreds of years. Many Americans today challenge this view, but 200 years ago attitudes were more entrenched.

Some Indian tribes, notably the Choctaws, Chickasaws, Seminoles, Creeks and Cherokees adopted the lifestyles and some of the culture of the white settlers and there was a lot of racial intermingling in frontier states like Tennessee.

Ironically much of the intermingling with the Indians came from the people who were the most hostile to the tribes - the Scots-Irish - in the years after the territorial boundaries were redrawn.

21

Warren Country *where the Scots-Irish settled*

Scots-Irish families were prominent in the settlement in the early 19th century of Warren County, on the western base of the Cumberland plateau in Tennessee. It is estimated that up to 75 per cent of Warren County's early settlers (1800-1840) were of Scots-Irish origin. They had moved to the region from the valley of Virginia and the Carolinas.

The County was established in 1807, taking its name from a patriot in the American Revolutionary War General Joseph Warren. McMinnville, the County capital about 100 miles from Nashville, was named after Joseph McMinn, a transplanted Pennslyvania Quaker and the then speaker of the Tennessee Senate.

The area which today comprises Warren County was generally recognised as the property of the Cherokee Indians until it officially came into the possession of the United States Government under the Third Treaty of Tellico in 1805. Frontier explorers had moved through the region from 1769, but it was not until 1805 that the white settlements became widely recognised.

The pioneering Scots-Irish found the territory of Warren County a wilderness: the valleys and coves were covered with an almost impenetrable growth of tall cane and the mountains and hills were laced with heavy timber. Game too was plentiful and how the frontiersmen relished the hunts for deer and bear. But the soil was fertile, the climate was healthy and water was in abundance. By the early 19th century the Indian tribes had been removed from the region and this was the signal for settlement to begin.

The first man to settle in the County was Elisha Pepper in 1800. He arrived, with his family, in the lands that today are McMinnville from the valley of Virginia. Elisha was Scots-Irish, a hardy soul who lived until he was 100 years of age. Other early settlers in the same locality were Andrew Gambhill, Lyon Mitchell, Joseph Colville, William North, John Davis, Doctors John Wilson and William P. Lawrence, William Lisk and Edward Hogue.

It is recorded that the men and women of the Scots-Irish tradition who came to McMinnville and the surrounding region of Warren County in the covered wagon migration were typical of and similar to the early settlers in other parts of Tennessee. Most were of honourable character, with a natural inkling for an advancement of their education and work base - solid Calvinistic ethics.

From its early days McMinnville was a town with an antebellum reputation for fine schools and an educated community. Some of Tennessee's foremost lawyers received their early tuition in McMinnville. Many of the early homes in the town - when the early log cabin era elapsed - were of brick , comfortable, commodious and dignified. No churches were erected in McMinnville until 1837. Prior to this, services of the various denominations were held in schools, and the first church erected in the town was a one-storey brick building belonging to the Primitive Baptists. Methodist, Presbyterian and Episcopal churches followed.

By 1833, when the town's population had reached 700, there were five lawyers locally, two academics, one school, a post office, three blacksmith shops, two bricklayers, five carpenters, five cabinet makers, two painters, one printing and newspaper office, six saddlers, five shoemakers, one silversmith, eight tailors, five tanners, two taverns and seven stores. There were also factories in operation for the manufacture of gun and pistol barrels, hoes, axes, mattocks, leather, chains and salt. By the standards in the then frontier, McMinnville was a very prosperous community.

Today the population of McMinnville is about 11,500, about half of the total for Warren County. It remains an extremely go-ahead township, with its people possessing all the vigour and enterprise of the founding fathers, to a large degree the Scots-Irish who erected a civilisation out of a timbered wilderness.

"Wherever the Ulster folk have gone, the breath of the North has followed them. Masterful and independent from the beginning, masterful and independent they remained; inflexible in purpose, impatient of injustice, and staunch in their ideals". - English historian, Henderson.

22

Music and Dance *that crossed the Atlantic*

The distinctive drone notes of some modern-day American country music performers can be traced directly back to the Scots-
Irish settlers of 200 years ago. And the dance tradition of the
Appalachian and Smoky Mountain region has also very strong Scots-
Irish roots. It is simplistic and inaccurate to interpret American country
music and dance as entirely Scots-Irish in influence, but there are certain elements of this tradition which are still to the fore on this scene
today. Bill Ivey, director of the American Country Music Foundation
in Nashville, and Jacky Christian, of the American Old Time Music and
Dance Foundation, verify this.

"The sounds of drone notes, associated with the pipes and fiddles are
very pronounced. The story telling elements of balladry of the Scots-
Irish also remains strong. They may not be as strong or dominant as
they were in the 1920s because country music, like blues and jazz, has
since come into contact with other forms of music," confirms Bill Ivey.

"But the roots of the Scots-Irish in country music are very pronounced.
One of the interesting things about country music is that it developed in
the South. There were Irish, Scottish and English settlers there who
brought their musical traditions across the Atlantic with them and this
culture blended with the Afro tradition.

"These connections and mixes were very important to what we think
of as country music today, just as the Anglo influence was very important in taking African music and making it into the blues. The blues is
African-influenced, but it is not African music.

"Even today, the Irish, Scottish and English influences are still flow-
ing into country music. For instance, if you listen to Ricky Skaggs - a
very, very professional performer who is involved in the Appalachian/
bluegrass tradition of country music, you will find that link. His nasel-
voiced styles and his fiddle playing are very traditional, closely connected with the Scots-Irish immigrants of 200 years ago. His approach
to performing styles and the close connection with folk music are also
apparent.

"I think you could contrast Ricky with someone like Garth Brooks,
who draws on a lot of pop music and western influences and would not
be connected so much with the Anglo tradition. But if you look generally at the spectrum of contemporary country music, some performers
are much closer to Scots-Irish influences than others. Emmylou Harris
is one - she is very close to these influences. The acoustic instruments
her band uses and the songs she sings are also in that tradition. And
there are also Bill Monroe and Jim and Jesse McReynolds, bluegrass
performers from the Scots-Irish tradition".

Bill Ivey says there are certain Scots-Irish elements which have stayed
part of country music, primarily the sound of drone notes that are associated with the bagpipes. "American country music is still essentially
'the whiteman's music' for down the years almost all the practitioners
have been white. The Anglo tratitions are the dominant themes, but the
gospel influences in country music are a blend of both white and black
traditions, based mainly on church life in the southern states".

Nashville's first lady of country music, Dolly Parton, brought up in
the Smoky Mountains, has strong Scots-Irish blood in her veins - her
father Robert Lee Parton could trace his roots back to the early settlers,
while her mother was of mixed origin, part Anglo, part Cherokee Indian. Many in the Appalachian region have some Indian connection. At
Dolly's East Tennessee theme park at Pigeon Forge, the musical docu-
mentary 'Fire On The Mountain' tells the fascinating story of American country music and its historical roots, particularly the Scots-Irish
connection. The musical narrative confirms the link: "And so they came
..... a strong willed people who forged their homes out of this region
and brought their love and beauty with them. The deeds of our Scots-
Irish ancestors are blended with the skills of the musicians who seized
the Smokies' fiery spirit and this heritage has been passed on from generation to generation .....!"

Dolly's grandfather Jake Owens was an "old-tyme" preacher man in the Great Smoky Mountains and a highly talented musician, her uncles Bill and Louis Owens confirm. "He taught music with old-tyme shape notes and the singing in his little Pentecostal church was a joy to behold. That's where Dolly started her musical career, as a child singer - she was following in a family tradition", says Bill.

"The songs we sing and play are essentially mountain music. It was music that was brought to these parts 200 years ago by the Scots, the Irish and German peoples. My family come from Scots-Irish descent and we even have a little Indian blood in our veins", adds Louis.

The Owens have a love of traditional fiddle, particularly the Irish fiddle tunes, some of which have been played in the Smokies since the late 18th century. The Scots-Irish tradition of dancing on toes is still very common today in Tennessee and surrounding states.

Jacky Christian confirms that the style of dance in the United States can be categorised into two main themes: first, the European dance customs which came from Ireland, Scotland and Wales in the 18th and 19th centuries, and second, the Afro dance customs of the Blacks.

"Just like the music they have blended over a period of time. But in the Appalachians some of the older European dance traditions have remained longer, largely because of the isolation of the region and the independent character of the people.

"The Irish, Scottish and English 'clogging' form of dancing blended over the years in the Appalachians, although there were slight variants from region to region, hill and hollar and one to another. You can easily detect the Scots-Irish roots in a community by the dances they do".

"There's a lot of instrument backing for the Scots-Irish forms of dance here and the dancers operate quite a bit on their toes, from a very erect still upper body movement. But as you get into the more Southern states there is a very Black culture, a slave culture, and you will find this dance is lower to the floor; the body position crouches and is more fluid.

"The square dance is the national dance and in the southern part of the United States there's a style called Appalachian square dance or Dix. The only musical backing is a fiddle, an instrument which is very Scots-Irish in origin. The fiddle was the first musical instrument in these parts 200 years ago. There might only have been one fiddle in a whole community, and one player".

John Rice Irwin, founder of the Appalachian Museum at Norris in East Tennessee, recounts that the heroes when he was growing up in the region were the old-time fiddlers.

"My great uncle Lee was one of the best fiddlers in the country and won contests in four or five states. No one made a living by being a musician in those days. Uncle Lee was a farmer, a hunter, a sort of historian; was very steady and direct and had a quick temper - the Scots-Irish in him.

"John Hartford, one of the greatest singers and instrumentalists in America today and who wrote 'Gentle on My Mind' the most recorded song in history, studied closely my Uncle Lee's fiddle playing. Roy Acuff, the acknowledged 'King of Country Music', came here one day and he listened to some of our music from the Smoky Mountains and Appalachians. We were sitting around pickin' away and Roy, who was about 85 at the time, said: 'You can't hear this kind of music in Nashville any more'.

"There is a direct link between country music and the music that left Ireland and Scotland 200 years ago. The music, as I heard it growing up here, came originally from the North of Ireland.

"I remember an old man by the name of Jim McCarroll - he was one of the great old fiddlers - and he came out with words that sounded as if he was directly from Ireland. I was always struck by it. Old Jim played all the old songs, tunes like the Green River March and The Knoxville Girl, songs that had origins in Ireland. Folk in this region, in the mountains, were not always conscious of where their ancestors came from.

"They had been moving from generation to generation and once they left Pennslyvania - they left their parents and grandparents over in Ireland to move here - they lost a lot of touch. Then they moved on a little more; when they moved down the Shenadoah Valley they lost more, and when they reached Tennessee it was as if they had dropped out of the sky.

"They had lost touch with the past for two reasons. They had families of 14 children; they were up in the morning early; out working in the fields; home tired late at night. It wasn't until later in life that they had some leisure time sitting on the porch that they managed to catch up with the past. From the time they left Ireland and kept moving they appeared to lose all contact with their original roots".

Ricky Skaggs is another top American country music star with very definite Ulster-Scots roots. "My family on my mother's side were Scots-Irish - they were the Fergusons who left Limavady and East Donegal for America in the early part of the 18th century. They eventually moved to Kentucky where I grew up with a real taste for bluegrass music which has its origins in the north of Ireland and Scotland. My family on my father's side are Scandinavian", says Ricky, like his wife Sharon White a committed Christian and respected member of the Grand Ole Opry in Nashville.

His roots in country music and gospel run deep: "To me, traditional country music has a value in it, a wholesomeness and warmth that some of the other kinds of music don't have. It's our heritage, our roots, it's everything that we're about. The music is very special to me and Sharon".

One Scots Irish family who left a rich musical legacy on the frontier were the McMichens. The first known ancestor of this line in America was John Hiram McMichen, who was born in Spartanburg, South Carolina in 1805. Hiram's father or grandfather left Ireland in the late 19th century and he married Jane Armstrong, who was born in Drung, Co. Cavan in Ireland. The family were originally Presbyterians, some became Methodists, but most joined with the Fundamentalist Universal Church.

The McMichens were among the finest "old-tyme" fiddlers in the Appalachian region and in the early part of this century Clayton McMichen dominated the bluegrass music scene, starring at the Grand Ole Opry, (the old Ryman Auditorium) in Nashville as a contemporary of Jimmie Rodgers, the father of American country music. Clayton died in 1970 in Kentucky, a celebrated figure in American country music.

Dr. Bill Foster, a professor of English at the University of North Alabama, is Scots-Irish and extremely proud of it. Along with his wife, daughter and son, he performs in a bluegrass band that had been voted the best string outfit in this category in the annual awards in Nashville.

'My ancestor came from the north of Ireland and he landed in Charleston, North Carolina about 1769 and headed west into the Appalachian mountains. He brought with him a fiddle which I inherited when I was 21 and supposedly it had been handed down to the eldest in my family with the saying: 'This is the fiddle that came from Ireland with the first one of our family who came to America'. I really treasure this fiddle. I have had it analysed and appraised and I happen to know that it is about 250 years old and that it is a fairly decent job of home-made fiddle".

Northern Ireland is one part of the world where American country music is very highly popular today. This is not surprising, considering the indelible links the Province has with the Appalachian region where American country music first took hold.

23

The ancient tradition *of Moonshine*

The practice of moonshining - illicit whiskey making - was intro
duced to America by the Scots-Irish when they began pouring
into the frontier lands in the 18th century. This ancient and illegal art had its origins in Scotland, in the 16th century. It was taken
across to the north of Ireland at the time of the Scottish plantation there
and it became a tradition in the Appalachian mountain region from about
1750 onwards.

Before they left Scotland and Ireland the Scots-Irish settlers were
forced to hide their small stills in wild and inaccessable places to avoid
the despised British tax collectors. It was generally felt by ordinary
people at the time that the distillation of the white mountain spirits was
a man's own business. He tilled the soil and grew his grain, so why
should he have to pay a tariff on the whiskey he made on his own land?

In the Appalachians, the moonshine liquor - whiskey and brandy -
was made from a wide variety of ingredients: barley, raisins, grapes,
dandelions, rye, corn, peaches, apples, plums, persimmons and toma-
toes. Apple brandy was in big demand, as was mead, a sweet wine dis-
tilled from honey.

Moonshine became readily available in America at the time of the
Revolutionary War and it is said that the Scots-Irish battalions -

General George Washington's favourites - were highly popular, not only for their fighting prowess, but for the potent home brew they could produce at a glance.

After the war, however, things changed and when the new Washington-led government brought in a whiskey tax there was a revolt by the small frontier farmers, most of them Scots-Irish, who had a few years earlier helped rout the British in the Revolutionary battles.

The frontiersmen had been converting a large amount of their grain into whiskey, and, with difficulties encountered in the wild terrain in transporting the harvest yield, they contended that their crops could only be marketed economically by distilling them into a more easily transportable form. In loud and angry protests there were threats that the mountain settlers would take up arms against the Government and for a time the "Whiskey Rebellion" had an unsettling effect on the fledgling nation's authority along the frontier.

From Western Pennsylvania to the Appalachian states of Tennessee, Kentucky, Virginia, West Virginia, Georgia and North and South Carolina moonshining became ingrained in the mountain man's culture and it was practised there long after it had virtually disappeared in other parts of the United States.

When alcoholic prohibition was imposed in the United States in 1920, illegal distillation re-surfaced in most states, but in southern Appalachia the practice had never been wiped out. This meant the region received much closer attention than had been the case over the previous 150 years - from both the authorities and outside predators.

This was a period when city criminal elements moved in on the scene and to a large extent their involvement ruined the reputation of the proud old-time mountaineering moonshiner, who, though he was in clear breach of the law, remained a Godfearing family man who took a lot of care in his work.

Moonshining existed in areas where the land was not very good - in the rugged Smoky Mountains in East Tennessee one could always manage to pick up a bottle of the clear stuff, often referred to as "white lightning". This contrasted with other parts of Tennessee like Maury County in the central belt where the land was much richer. There the Scots-Irish settlers were among the first producers of Bourbon whiskey and today it is a highly lucrative industry in the region.

Maury County always had a much richer corn crop and, with limestone water readily available locally, the whiskey makers were able to lower the pH and take the acid out of the substance. This resulted in a smooth cinnamon whiskey which is now marketed as Bourbon.

Moonshining still exists in a much smaller measure in the Appalachian region, and in a few isolated parts of Northern Ireland and Scotland, from whence the art came. It remains a totally illegal preoccupation and the close attention of the police and customs has meant that the numbers of those operating underground stills are greatly reduced.

American talepiece of "The Sash"

Irish Mollyo was a song widely popular in North America in the late 18th and early 19th century, sung to the tune of the famous Orange party tune "The Sash My Father Wore."

The song was published by A. W. Auner of Philadelphia around 1830 and it was while digging through some old songs in the snowy Pokonos region of Pennsylvania recently that Northern Ireland folk singer Tommy Sands came across this Scots-Irish musical gem. It had obviously been taken across the Atlantic by the Scots-Irish settlers.

According to Tommy, the song lay dormant for more than 100 years and it spawned not only "The Hat My Father Wore" and "The Sash My Father Wore" but it also provided Beethoven with a theme for the first movement of his piano concerto number one.

A later Irish Mollyo emerged this century, but it was a completely different song. The original Irish Mollyo (sung to "The Sash") is to be released on an album by Tommy Sands on his Elm Grove Music label, Rostrevor, Co. Down.

Its words are:

"Tell me who is that poor stranger that lately came to town
And like a pilgrim all alone he wanders up and down
He's a poor forlorn Glasgow lad and if you would like to know
His heart is breaking all in vain for Irish Mollyo

Chorus:
She is young and she is beautiful and her likes I've never known
The lily of old Ireland and the primrose of Tyrone
She's the lily of old Ireland and no matter where I go
My heart will always hunger for my Irish Mollyo

Ah but when her father heard of this a solemn vow he swore
That if she wed a foreigner he'd never see her more
He called for young MacDonald and plainly told him so
I'll never give to such as you my Irish Mollyo

MacDonald heard the heavy news and sadly he did say
Farewell my lovely Molly I am banished far away
Til death shall come to comfort me and to the grave I go
My heart will always hunger for my Irish Mollyo"

• "The Sash" is a song associated with the cause of King William of Orange

24

Stone fences *as in Ulster*

S tone fences litter the landscape of Tennessee, Virginia and Kentucky today in the same way as they do in the northern part of Ireland. This is not a coincidence, but a tradition which was taken across the Atlantic by the Scots-Irish settlers.

The early Appalachian settlers not only built stone fences, but when they became established in a region they moved from log cabin homes to formidable stone dwellings, erected either by themselves or kinsfolk who were into masonry. The use of stone for houses and fences was a particular trait of the Scots-Irish families who moved through the Shenandoah valley of Virginia towards the bluegrass country of Kentucky and rich lands of middle Tennessee in the late 18th century.

Stone masonry is a trade that has been practised in Ireland and Scotland since the early ages and the dry laid limestone fences which began appearing on the early American frontier were erected by men who learned their basic skills back in the old countries. Comprehensive studies of stone house sites in the Appalachians confirm that the incidence of stone houses and rock fences is significantly higher at settlements belonging to the descendants of Scots-Irish settlers.

On these type of rock fences there is a tendency to place the bigger stones lengthways, along the face of the work and not across the wall. They can also be identified by a coping of mortar and, distinctively, the small stones are loosely placed on top of the fence, not built into it. Rock fences are still very common in the more hilly parts of Counties Down, Tyrone, Antrim, Londonderry and Donegal.

WAGONS

In 1775 a Presbyterian minister stood in the valley of Virginia and observed a migration of a people intent of starting a new life on the frontier. "We see many every day travelling to Carolina, some on foot with packs, and some in large covered wagons. The road here is much frequented", declared the preacher.

The wagons, known as the "North Carolina" wagons were said to be built in the manner of an ancient battle ship: a dip in the middle and the rear built much higher than the front.

"The high back was intended as a precaution against robbers as well as protection against a lurking foe. The tar bucket and one dog were tied to the rear axle, while the remainder of the pack followed. The lead horse and sometimes others had bells on them. These seemed to add cheer to all the caravan.

"When the horses were hitched and the bells began to tinkle the dogs leaped in delight that the day's journey was to begin again. The cattle were nearly always driven behind the wagons. Bells were tied to them too, and unless in case of men outriders, the horses with the packs followed the wagons too" - report from Historic Sullivan (Tennessee County). The settlers followed the trails established by Indians, long hunters, traders and animals.

THE FRONTIER WOMAN

In the annals of all countries there is no age nor race that has given to the world more sterling valour than that displayed by the frontier woman of Tennessee. She shared with the men all the dangers of the wilderness, with all its toils. She came with the first settlers and bore with fortitude the privations of a forest cabin.

"No other border life of recent times, in our territories, presents such a wonderful growth and change from wild backwoods to the dignity of a state in 26 years. To her presence more than any one influence, to her moral worth and example, is due the high rank attained and the end achieved in so short a time. She did not wait for the clearing and the building of the cabin and the planting of the crops - she went along and helped do these things.

"She rocked the cradle in the home - she swung the cradle in the field. She spun the flax and carded the wool and made the clothing for the family. She has gone to the aid of the sick neighbor and returned to find her own home in ashes. When rumours of Indian raids reached the settlements she went into the fort prepared to do a man's part should the exigency of the hour demand. In such a test of courage she stood, gun in hand, beside the dead body of the man who had fallen, the victim of a besieger's bullet. And still the mother's thoughtful care over her children never left her. She trained them at her knee. The frontier woman of Tennessee never lacked for courage nor opportunities to prove it.

"There was a peculiar trait which seemed to be born in the children of that day, or which mothers had taught them - to make no show of fear nor make alarm, much like the young birds, which, at a call, seek the cover of the wing. It was a hush of caution rather than of fear.

* **from *Historic Sullivan, Tennessee*. by Oliver Taylor.**

EARLY AMERICAN PROVINCIAL OR STATE GOVERNORS OF ULSTER BIRTH OR EXTRACTION

James Logan: 1674: Pennsylvania
John McKinley: 1721: Delaware
John Hancock: 1737: Massachusetts
Thomas Nelson: 1738: Virginia
George Clinton: 1739: New York
John Rutledge: 1739: South Carolina
Edward Rutledge: 1749: South Carolina
Jeremiah Smith: 1759: New Hampshire
John Bell: 1765: New Hampshire
Samuel Dinsmoor: 1768: Pennsylvania
William Findlay: 1768: Pennsylvania
De Witt Clinton: 1769: New York
Jeremiah Morrow: 1770: Ohio
Samuel Bell: 1770: New Hampshire
James Miller: 1776: Arkansas
Joseph Reid: 1778: Pennsylvania
Andrew Pickens: 1779: South Carolina
Allen Trimble: 1783: Ohio
Patrick Noble: 1787: South Carolina
Charles Polk: 1788: Delaware
Joseph M. Harper: 1789: New Hampshire
William Patterson: 1790: New Jersey
Robert P. Dunlap: 1794: Maryland
William L. Ewing: 1795: Illinois
John M. Patton: 1797: Virginia
Samuel Dinsmoor:1799: Pennsylvania
Thomas McKean: 1799: Pennsylvania
Hugh J. Anderson: 1801: Maryland
Noah Martin: 1801: New Hampshire
Robert M. Patton: 1809: Alabama
John B. Cochran: 1809: Delaware
Samuel W. Black: 1815: Nebraska
Peter H. Bell: 1812: Texas
James W. Grimes: 1816: Pennsylvania
William E. Stevenson: 1820: West Virginia
Charles H. Bell: 1823: New Hampshire

The dates are of birth.

25

Settlement *in the Sumner County*

Sumner County in middle Tennessee is a region where many Scots-Irish settlers settled and moved through after passing over the Cumberland Gap in Kentucky. They had come from Pennsylvania and Virgina, by-passing the large Indian settlements on the Ohio River and heading along the Shenandoah Valley.

The land in Sumner County, used only by the Indian tribes as hunting ground, was good and it was even better further along middle Tennessee at Maury County. During the last 20 years of the 18th century this frontier region became heavily populated by Scots-Irish Presbyterians and their influences have been manifest throughout the mainstream of society there since.

Sumner County, close to Nashville, was founded in 1787 and is the second oldest county in Tennessee, next to Davidson County which was established in 1783. The Indian tribes strongly resisted the movement of the white settlers into middle Tennessee and there were many bloody exchanges in the years leading up to 1794 when hostilities ceased in Sumner and the adjoining Davidson County.

The region had for centuries been the bread basket for the various Indian tribes - the Cherokees, the Shawnee, the Creeks, the Chickasaws and the Choctaws - and it was quite natural for them to violently resist the advances of the settlers. The methods used, on both sides, were savage with the frontiersmen quickly adapting to ruthless tactics used by the natives. It was the survival of the strongest and in time the white settlers succeeded in pushing the Indians back.

In 1786 the Avery Trace, a roadway linking East Tennessee and Middle Tennessee, was built with Sumner County and its main township of Gallatin, a strategic point between the two cities of Knoxville and Nashville. Today Gallatin has a population of about 20,000.

The Sumner County settlement can be traced back to several frontier stations built by white settlers. In 1784, Colonel Anthony Bledsoe built a fort on a tract of 6,280 acres, a grant he received for services in surveying during the Revolutionary War. In the same year General Daniel Smith laid the foundation to his new home near present Hendersonville on a land grant given to him for his services in the Revolutionary War. In 1785 John Shelby was born near Bledsoe's Lick and is thus thought to be the first white child born in Sumner County. He was the son of David and Sarah Bledsoe Shelby. His father was a Revolutionary War veteran and his mother a daughter of Colonel Anthony and Mary Ramsay Bledsoe. John Shelby later became a prominent citizen of Nashville. Shelby Street in that city is named after him.

About two and a half miles north of Greenfield on Bledsoe Creek, John Morgan and his son Captain John Morgan, in 1786, erected Morgan's Fort. It was located on the west side of the creek near the mouth of the Dry Fork on a tract of 640 acres granted to Captain Morgan for services in the Revolutionary War.

The Morgans had come to Sumner County in 1785 with Revolutionary War Major William Hall, whose oldest daughter, Mary married Captain John Morgan. Captain Morgan moved to Fayetteville, Tennessee, in 1803, and raised a company of mounted troops which served with General Andrew Jackson in the Creek War. Like many of his compatriots, he and his family had suffered at the hands of the Indians. Although advanced in years at the time of the Creek War, he is reported to have said, "A man should never get too old to fight the British and Indians."

Hamilton's fort, also known as the ridge station, was built in 1788 at the head of Drake's Creek on the highland rim, five or six miles north of Shackle Island in Sumner County. The fort was built after Indians attacked and killed the three young Montgomery brothers - John, Robert and Thomas. Settlers near the fort had come out largely from the nearby Mansker's station and believed the Indian troubles were over. Thomas Hamilton's land was on the site of the fort. Hamilton, of Ulster-Scots descent, had fought throughout the American Revolution and was said to be "as brave a man as ever took a gun or sword in hand."

Scots-Irish Presbyterians were most numerous among the early settlers of Sumner County and the Shiloh Presbyterian Church about five miles from Gallatin was the first place of worship in the area. It was formed in 1793 by the Rev. William McGee, who was attached to the Muhlenburg Presbytery, and Presbyterians worshipped there for more than 150 years. The congregation is no longer, but in recent years the church has been restored by Presbyterians from Gallatin. First Presbyterian Church in Gallatin was established in 1828 and still plays a prominent role in the life of Sumner County.

Methodists appeared in Sumner County about 1790 when a number of "societies" were formed to pray and testify to each other of their personal religious belief and experience. It was to such groups that the circuit riding preacher came and preached and in the early years Methodism strongly rivalled Presbyterianism in the area.

VALLEY OF VIRGINIA

German Lutherans were the first immigrants to inhabit the Shenandoah valley of Virginia, driven from their homes in the Rhenish Palatine and Wurtemburg regions of Germany by the ravages of French invaders and the harsh economic conditions prevailing in Europe then.

On the heels of the Germans there came to the Great Valley in more numerous numbers a continuing tide of immigrants from the British Isles, much of it made up of Scots-Irish Presbyterians. In the historical annals of The Southern Appalachians (The Discoverers) it is related that the Scots-Irish followed much the same path as the Germans.

"Landing at northeastern ports, they made their way to the hinterlands of New York and Pennsylvania, whence those who could not find land within their means turned south into The Great Valley. Filtering down through the mountains, they met other English and Scots Presbyterians from the Piedmont area of South Carolina, whose experiences of the privileges enjoyed by the Anglican Church and the planter aristocracy had given them a similar rebellious outlook.

" These new Americans were fiercely independent, equalitarian and self-reliant, possessed of an indomitable will to survive and prevail, tough in mind and body. Stung by the slights and injuries they had taken from the advantaged class, their superiors in breeding, cultivation and wealth, they were hostile to all that class stood for. They were bound by no ties to the Old World or like their German fellows, to the English Crown.

"With a stern, fatalistic religion to keep their impetuosity in check, the Scots-Irish combined an intense and ingenious practicality, shrewdness and a long grasp for life's tangibles. From their habituation to clan warfare in the ancestral home and to battling the wild Celts in Ulster, they brought with them a fighting instinct and aggressiveness and a handiness with weapons. Given the nature of the American frontier and the general determination to advance it, regardless, they made ideal frontiersmen, the equal before long of the Redmen, whose woodcraft and dress they adopted. They were not only the new Americans, they were to be the creators of the New America. This would formally suceed to the old when one of their number, Andrew Jackson, was elected to the Presidency. And of this New America, which would sweep westward to the Pacific in the course of the next century, southern Appalachia was a prime staging area."

26

Scots-Irish *with loyalist sympathies*

Alexander Chesney was a typical Ulster-Scots Presbyterian on the American frontier who differed from most of his fellow countrymen and co-religionists in that he fought for the British Crown in the Revolutionary War.

Chesney, born in 1756 at Dunlug in Co. Antrim in the area that today forms part of the town of Ballymena, was in the army of Colonel Patrick Ferguson at the battle of Kings Mountain on October 7, 1780. Alexander's father was Robert McChesney (the family dropped the " MC" shortly after reaching America) and his mother was Jane Fulton. His brothers and sisters married into the families of Purdy, Gillespey, Archbold, Wilson, Symonton, Cook, Nisbet, Peden, Grier, Wylie, McJunkin, McCleland. Barclay, Pogue, Phillips and Brandon, all of whom came to be located in the area of South Carolina.

Chesney and his mother, father, three brothers, and four sisters sailed from Larne aboard a small ship named James and Mary on August 25, 1772. After a voyage of seven weeks and three days, they reached Charleston, South Carolina. Although they were weary of the cramped space on the little vessel, they were not allowed to land.

Smallpox was aboard the ship and the authorities made the ship and some of its passengers ride at anchor for 52 days. Those sick with smallpox were removed from the vessel and housed on Sullivan's Island. When everyone was declared clean of the dreaded desease, they were allowed to come ashore at Prichard's shipyard on Town Creek, a few miles above Charleston. None of them were allowed to enter town. Fortunately, the Chesney family knew where they were heading because members of their family had earlier reached the frontier and had sent written word of the availability of land.

Once inland, Chesney and his father reached an agreement with John Millar, of Turkey Creek, to transport and leave the mother and the younger children with John Winn at Winnsboro, South Carolina while they went to their relatives to obtain help in moving the family further inland. After the father and son departed it was discovered that Millar was too old and infirm to carry out the agreement. At that point, John Phillips, a kinsman by marriage, agreed to fetch the Chesney family as far inland as his own home. Phillips agreed to pay Winn one penny per pound of the combined weight of the small children and the furnishings for the hire of his wagon. Later in the American Revolutionary War, Winn and Phillips served as colonels on opposite sides.

The Chesneys obtained 100 acres near the home of Phillips, cleared a spot, and erected a small cabin. However, they received a letter from Sarah Cook, a widowed kinswoman, entreating them to come and settle as her neighbour. The family dispatched Alexander, the oldest son, to travel the 60 miles to the home of Mrs. Cook to decide whether they should abandon the work they had invested or remain where they were. Alexander did not have a horse and there was not a road thet led to Grindal Shoals. By walking through the woods in the direction he supposed Grindal Shoals to be, he came to the house of John Quin, a blacksmith, on Sandy River. From there he went to the home of Ned Neil on Broad River. He crossed the river by canoe and thence up the Pacolet River to the home of Eliza Wells. Here, he learned he was five miles from the home of Mrs. Cook, his aunt.

With the aid of his cousins, the Cook family, and Charles Brandon, a cousin by marriage, he found 400 acres of suitable land and had it surveyed in the name of his father. Chesney moved to Charleston and obtained title to the land and then returned to move the family to Grindal Shoals. While their new home was being built, the family resided with Mrs Cook. Eventually, the Chesney family settled on their own land on the north side of the Pacolet River near Grindal Shoals and about 12 miles from where the Pacolet and Broad Rivers joined. Here the family resided from 1773.

But the peace and harmony which all the settlers of the Carolinas treasured was about to be shattered and the Chesneys, being loyal to King George 111 of England, were in the front line.

27

An *American view*

T he tale of the Ulster-Scot heritage in America is, in my opinion, "the greatest story never told".

British tax and Presbyterian church records show my family at Tobergill outside Donegore in the vicinity of Templepatrick in Co. Antrim at the time of the Hearth and Head Rolls of the 1660s. Persecuted as religious "dissenters" this planter family from the Scottish borders migrated on to the British fort of New Castle in the 1770s in what would later become the State of Delaware. Hugh Scott his wife and family were founding members of the Presbyterian Church, U.S.A, and Hugh Scott's own grandson, named after his grandfather, became a Major in America's fight for Independence and was also a founding elder in the first Presbyterian Church west of the Alleghany Mountains in western Pennsylvania.

Indeed, George Washington, said that if the famous winter at Valley Forge had decimated the American Army he would have gone into the mountains with the Ulster/Scots to carry on a guerrilla campaign against the British. The second Hugh Scott is my sixth-great grandfather, who, along with his wife, is still buried in the little graveyard of Pidgeon Creek Presbyterian Church, which he helped found in 1782.

The Ulster/Scots, or the Scotch-Irish as they are known in the United States, vanished from the telling of American history and literature as quickly as they blended into the western frontier along the Appalachian mountain chain, the first natural obstacle to colonial America's desire to go west. Having no love for the English, the Ulster/Scot moved quickly away from the seaports on the eastern seaboard to become God's frontiersmen - pioneers and Indian fighters during North America's French-Indian Wars.

As early American settlers who were the first Europeans to move to the frontier the Ulster/Scot's ethnic identity has never been popularly celebrated in either literature or drama - we were one of the first British folkwaves on the shores of the New World, the others were the Puritans in the North East and the Cavaliers in the tidewater of Virginia and the Carolinas. Plain spoken with simple lifestyles, they were to greet, or just as often argue, with the successive waves of later ethnic migrations from Europe in the 18th, 19th and 20th centuries.

I have visited Northern Ireland six times in the last three years. Invariably, during my conversations there the subject of the anonymity of the Ulster/Scots in American history comes to the surface. It's a mystery. Perhaps, someday, someone in America will produce a film on this untold story.

Robert L. Scott, MARIETTA, GEORGIA, USA, June, 1995

28

Belfast, *Tennessee*

Belfast, Tennessee unlike Belfast, Northern Ireland is only a small hamlet with a general store around which live a few hundred inhabitants.

Once the disputed hunting grounds of several Indian tribes, Belfast was first settled in 1807 by Scots-Irish veterans of the Revolutionary War, who received the land in payment of their services. William Williams first opened his Belfast store in 1808 at the foot of Round Hill. In 1829, the store was moved to what is called " Old Belfast" when Williams purchased an inn, a tavern and adjacent farm land at what is now the intersections of Finley-Beech and Belfast-Farmington (Highway 271) Road.

The " Robert Williams General Merchandise Store" moved to its present location in 1878 following the completion of the Duck River Valley Railroad. In 1894, J.C. Tate began operating the business which bore his name until the death of his son, Ed Tate, in 1991, making it the oldest, continuously operated business in the state of Tennessee.

Reopened on Country Store Day, May 1, 1993, the Belfast General Store is now operated by Walter W, and Sigrid Holley Hedge and features art work by Sigrid, one of Appalachia's leading visionary artists. The Belfast Store offers a large selection of gifts and collectibles as well as unique handcraft items by Tennessee artisans.

Highway 271 lies of the main route from Nashville to Birmingham, Alabama.

Ulster *place names*

The settlement of the Scots-Irish immigrants in the United States is underlined by a profusion of Northern Ireland place names. There are 18 towns in the States named Belfast, including one in Tennessee; seven Derrys, nine Antrims and 16 Tyrones. There is a Coleraine in Massachusetts; a Stewartstown in New Hampshire. Washington, Ohio and Iowa have each a Pomeroy; Hillsborough is in New Hampshire, Illinois, North Dakota and Wisconsin. Maine has a Newry, Ohio a Banbridge and in 12 states there is a Milford. In Michigan, there is a town named after the Battle of the Boyne and in Cumberland County in the Carolinas there are townships of Antrim, Derry, Fermanagh and Tyrone. Ulster place names litter the landscape of the United States.

29

States *of the Union*

Tennessee became the 16th state of the American Union on June 1, 1796, exactly four years to the day after Kentucky was officially designated a state. In 1790 Tennessee had a registered population of 35,691 and by 1800 this had increased to 105,602; by 1810 261,727 and by 1850 it was as high as 1,002,717. Today the Tennessee population is five million.

ADMISSION OF STATES TO THE UNION:

1	Delaware	*Dec. 7, 1787*
2	Pennsylvania	*Dec. 12, 1787*
3	New Jersey	*Dec. 18, 1787*
4	Georgia	*Jan. 2, 1788*
5	Connecticut	*Jan. 9, 1788*
6	Massachusetts	*Feb. 6, 1788*
7	Maryland .	*Apr. 28, 1788*
8	South Carolina	*May 23, 1788*
9	New Hampshire	*June 21, 1788*
10	Virginia	*June 25, 1788*
11	New York	*July 26, 1788*
12	North Carolina	*Nov. 21, 1789*
13	Rhode Island	*May 29, 1790*
14	Vermont	*Mar. 4, 1791*
15	Kentucky	*June 1, 1792*
16	Tennessee	*June 1, 1796*
17	Ohio	*Mar. 1, 1803*
18	Louisiana	*Apr. 30, 1812*
19	Indiana	*Dec. 11, 1816*

20	Mississippi	*Dec. 10, 1817*
21	Illinois	*Dec. 3, 1818*
22	Alabama	*Dec. 14, 1819*
23	Maine	*Mar. 15, 1820*
24	Missouri	*Aug. 10, 1821*
25	Arkansas	*June 15, 1836*
26	Michigan	*Jan. 26, 1837*
27	Florida	*Mar. 3, 1845*
28	Texas	*Dec. 29, 1845*
29	Iowa	*Dec. 28, 1846*
30	Wisconsin	*May 29, 1848*
31	California	*Sept. 9, 1850*
32	Minnesota	*May 11, 1858*
33	Oregon	*Feb. 14, 1859*
34	Kansas	*Jan. 29, 1861*
35	West Virginia	*June 19, 1863*
36	Nevada	*Oct. 31, 1864*
37	Nebraska	*Mar. 1, 1867*
38	Colorado	*Aug. 1, 1876*
39	North Dakota	*Nov. 2, 1889*
40	South Dakota	*Nov. 2, 1889*
41	Montana	*Nov. 8, 1889*
42	Washington	*Nov. 11, 1889*
43	Idaho	*July 3, 1890*
44	Wyoming	*July 10, 1890*
45	Utah	*Jan. 4, 1896*
46	Oklahoma	*Nov. 16, 1907*
47	New Mexico	*Jan. 6, 1912*
48	Arizona	*Feb. 14, 1912*
49	Alaska	*Jan. 3, 1959*
50	Hawaii	*Aug. 21, 1959*

• *In the case of the first 13 states, the date given is that of ratification of the Constitution.*

30

Counties *of Tennessee*

Tennessee has 95 counties in its three regions - east, middle and west.

EAST TENNESSEE:

1777	Washington	1836	Bradley
1779	Sullivan	1836	Meigs
1783	Greene	1839	Polk
1787	Hawkins	1844	Hancock
1792	Jefferson	1849	Scott
1792	Knox	1850	Union
1794	Sevier	1855	Cumberland
1795	Blount	1870	Hamblen
1796	Grainger	1870	Loudon
1796	Carter	1875	Unicoi
1797	Cocke		
1801	Anderson		
1801	Roane		
1801	Claiborne		
1806	Campbell		
1807	Rhea		
1807	Bledsoe		
1817	Morgan		
1817	Marion		
1819	McMinn		
1819	Monroe		
1819	Hamilton		
1836	Johnson		

MIDDLE TENNESSEE:

1783 Davidson	1817 Wayne
1787 Sumner	1817 Lawrence
1796 Robertson	1819 Perry
1796 Montgomery	1823 Fentress
1799 Wilson	1836 Cannon
1799 Smith	1836 Marshall
1799 Williamson	1836 Coffee
1801 Jackson	1837 DeKalb
1803 Dickson	1840 Van Buren
1803 Stewart	1842 Macon
1803 Rutherford	1843 Lewis
1806 Overton	1844 Grundy
1806 White	1854 Putnam
1807 Warren	1856 Cheatham
1807 Bedford	1857 Sequatchie
1807 Franklin	1870 Trousdale
1807 Hickman	1870 Clay
1807 Maury	1871 Moore
1809 Humphreys	1871 Houston
1809 Lincoln	1879 Pickett
1809 Giles	

WEST TENNESSEE:

1819 Hardin	1823 Obion
1819 Shelby	1823 Tipton
1821 Henry	1823 Haywood
1821 Carroll	1824 Fayette
1821 Madison	1835 Benton
1821 Henderson	1835 Lauderdale
1823 McNairy	1845 Decatur
1823 Hardeman	1870 Lake
1823 Dyer	1871 Crockett
1823 Gibson	1879 Chester
1823 Weakley	

Acknowlegements

Barbara Parker, Department of Tourist Development, Nashville.
John Rice-Irwin, Museum of Appalachia, Norris, Tennessee.
David Babelay, East Tennessee Historical Society, Knoxville.
Dr Charles L. and Sara Moffatt, Gallatin, Tennessee.
Alton Kelley, Columbia, Maury County, Tennessee.
Dr Ian Adamson, Deputy Lord Mayor, Belfast.
David Wright (Artist), Nashville.
Ronnie Hanna, Ulster Society, Banbridge, County Down.
Dr Bobby Moss, Blacksburg, South Carolina.
Lorene Lambert, Department of Tourist Development, Nashville.
Dr. Robert E. Rhea, Kingston Springs, Tennessee.
Bill Ivey, Country Music Foundation, Nashville.
Jacky Christian, Old Time Music and Dance Foundation, Nashville.
Fred Brown, Knoxville News Sentinel.
Robert L. Scott, Ulster\American Co., Atlanta, Georgia.
Captain Carl Netherland-Brown, Rogersville, Tennessee.
Herb Roberts, Sycamore Shoals, Elizabethton, Tennessee.
Dr. Richard Blaustein, East Tennessee State University, Johnson City.
John Gilmour, Ulster-American Folk Park, Omagh, County Tyrone.
Dr Thomas W. Burton, East Tennessee State University, Johnson City.
George E. Webb, Books and Autographs, Rogersville,Tennessee.
Joe Costley, Belfast.
Stephen Cox,Tennessee State Museum.
David Logsdon, The Nashville Banner, Tennessee.
Caneta Hankins, Historic Preservation Centre, Murfreesboro, Tennessee.
Geoff Martin, Editor, Ulster/Belfast News Letter

Brian Courtney, Portadown, County Armagh.
Sharon McPherson, The Hermitage, Nashville.
John Garrott, Gallatin, Tennessee
Gary and Terry Kennedy, Portadown, County Armagh.
Robert Anderson, Richhill, County Armagh.
Bill and Louis Owens, Dollywood, Pigeon Forge, Tennessee.
Dr Bill Foster, University of North Alabama.
Charles G. Hurst, Birmingham, Alabama.
Michael McCombe, Librarian, Ulster/Belfast News Letter.
Tommy Sands, (folklorist), Rostrevor, Co. Down.
Elizabeth Queener, Nashville.
Pat McColgan, Belfast.

Pictures and Illustrations

Museum of Appalachia, Norris, Tennessee.
Barbara Parker, Department of Tourist Development, Nashville.
Cecil McCausland, Ulster News Letter.
Aubrey Watson, Nashville, Tennessee.
Alton Kelley, Columbia, Maury County, Tennessee.
David Babelay, Knoxville.
Dr Charles L. Moffatt, Gallatin, Tennessee.
First Knoxville Presbyterian Church.
The Hermitage, Nashville.
University of East Tennessee, Knoxville.
Zion Presbyterian Church, Columbia, Maury County.
United States Capitol Historical Society.
Image of John Rhea: Tennessee State Museum Collection, Nashville, Tennessee
Image of Sam Houston: Tennessee State Museum, Tennessee Historical Society Collection, Nashville, Tennessee.

Thanks

I would gratefully acknowledge the tremendous help and assistance given to me in compiling this book by so many people in the United States.

From across the Appalachian region and from other American states I have received a shoal of information on the Scots-Irish families who settled on the frontier 200/250 years. I fully appreciate the time and effort taken by those to whom the Scots-Irish tradition and culture means so much and I greatly value the many letters of support sent to me for this project. I hope that through this book many more people will come to know and understand the sacrifices made by a strong resolute people in creating a civilisation and a structured way of life in a wilderness. The United States would not be the nation it is today had it not been for the pioneering spirit of the Scots-Irish. Their valour and outstanding achievements make them a very special people.

Billy Kennedy

The author can be contacted at:

49 Knockview Drive,
Tandragee,
Craigavon,
Northern Ireland,
BT62 2BH

Bibliography

- Stories of the Great West - Theodore Roosevelt
- The Scotch-Irish, A Social History - James G. Leyburn
- Ulster Sails West - W.F. Marshall
- Land of the Free, Ulster and the American Revolution - Ronnie Hanna
- Religion in Tennessee 1777-1945 - Herman A. Norton
- The Overmountain Men - Pat Alderman
- One Heroic Hour at Kings Mountain - Pat Alderman
- With Fire and Sword - Wilma Dykeman
- Ulster Emigration to Colonial America - R.J. Dickson
- Houston and Crockett, Heroes of Tennessee and Texas - An Anthology.
- Samuel Doak (1749-1830) - William Gunn Calhoun
- Samuel Doak - by Earle W. Crawford
- The Wataugans - Max Dixon
- Historic Sullivan County, Tennessee - Oliver Taylor
- For Christ in the Heart of Knoxville (History of Knoxville's First Presbyterian Church) - Ashley Mack
- Patriots at Kings Mountain - Bobby Gilmer Moss
- The Long Rifle - Robert Lagemann and Albert C. Manucy
- America's First Western Frontier, East Tennessee - Brenda G. Calloway
- Alex Stewart - Portrait of a Pioneer - John Rice Irwin
- Knox County, Tennessee - Betsey Beeler Creekmore
- The Friersons of Zion Church - Theodore Frierson Stephenson
- Belfast News Letter, 250 Years (1737-1987)
- Andrew Jackson's Hermitage

- Zion Presbyterian Church, Columbia, Tennessee
- Knoxville's First Graveyard 1800-1879 (East Tennessee Historical Society)
- Mary Patton, Powder Maker of the Revolution - Robert A. Howard and E. Alvin Gerhardt Jnr
- A Precarious Belonging, Presbyterians and the Conflict in Ireland - John Dunlop (Blackstaff Press).

The author has sought to credit, where possible, all his sources, but should he have inadvertently overlooked anyone it is hoped that this will be understood.

Index